D1214714

Abstracts and Images

Lee Andersen

Lee is a New Zealander with a talented knitter for a mother.

She was brought up believing a house full of colourful yarn was normal and that knitting was just something that came off the needles. Her mother knitted whatever was necessary for the constantly accumulating children around her. (Lee is one of six and now there are grand children ...)

After completing a Bachelor of Education majoring in Art and a three year Diploma of Teaching, Lee began painting and exploring wearable art and, naturally, knitting surfaced as a medium.

When the designs started coming faster than her fingers could knit she began working with other knitters in New Zealand until over 100 of the best were working straight from her drawings.

Her gallery Vibrant Handknits in Wellington, New Zealand supplied "one only " garments to "the rich, the famous and the royal" from around the world for six years.

Then in 1988 Lee fell in love! Unfortunately, Al lived in a different country (the U.S.) and knitting needles and coloured pencils are mobile. Lee moved.

"You Knit, Unique", her first book, teaches knitters how to design and offers humourous but practical solutions to those inevitable mishaps.

"You and Yours" features sweaters for both men and women or as Lee would say "who ever gets out of bed first in the morning."

"Reflections of You" has sweaters for the children in your life and includes instructions for knitting from their art work.

"EXTRA-Ordinary You" is a book of dramatic designs for the full figured female.

"The Casual You" presents contemporary designs for the family.

Lee's second gallery Vibrant Handknits USA has opened at Historic Savage Mill a restored eighteenth century textile mill in Savage, Maryland, a delightfully unique artist's marketplace and antique center.

The Plymouth Yarn Company, Inc.

presents

in
Cotton Soft
Galway & Encore

Lee Andersen

Edited by Joan Becker

Published by Vibrant Handknits, USA, Inc.
for The Plymouth Yarn Co, Inc.
P.O. Box 28, Bristol, Pennsylvania 19007 USA
Phone: 215-788-0459

4

Introduction

by Joan Becker

Creativity is problem solving. Designers often choose problems with very rigid specifications in order to stimulate the creative response. This is where Lee Andersen excels because she loves designing her way out of even the tightest corners.

Lee claims brief chaos is a necessary phase in the creative process. We have been friends for years and I can assure you that she is better at creating chaos than anyone I know. She uses new yarns in much the same way she uses paint on a new canvas - as an opportunity to make something where there is nothing. Lee 'sees' the beauty in new and ever changing color groups. As she adds her own emotional response to that color and translates it into lines and spaces, a unique exciting design unfolds.

Her love of the creative process led to this sixth book. The new 1200 sq ft sweater gallery at Historic Savage Mill in Maryland, 'Vibrant Handknits USA Inc.' (a joint venture for us) is successfully establishing a loyal following. Lee's original business 'Vibrant Handknits, New Zealand' is doing well and sending us beautiful "one of a kind" garments knitted straight from Lee's drawings. The samples of Lee's Signature Series designs for fall '94 look great. Life was just too dull for Lee's natural level of 'Hectivity'. She needed a new project.

During a chat with Plymouth Yarn Company, it was decided that Lee might have some fun with their three basic worsted weight yarns, Galway (a wool), Encore (a machine washable blend), and Cotton Soft (a cotton). "These yarns, all these yarns and only these yarns", extolled Plymouth management.

As many of you know Lee's "originals" and Signature Series sweaters and coats (each signed and numbered) usually have twenty or more colours and combine many different textured yarns. The design problem (or 'opportunity for creativity' as Lee would say) was the limitation of only three yarns, all smooth and all knitting at five stitches to the inch.

For you, the knitter, there are three advantages.
1) Most patterns are interchangable. Choose the yarn type you prefer, the instructions will be the same.
2) All the yarns are very affordable.
3) The same colours come up throughout the book so leftovers can go straight into another pattern.

This book is intended to be both practical and inspirational. Some of Lee's signature series designs which sell in the gallery are also included in the book because knitters often ask if patterns are available. The degree of difficulty for these garments was not a consideration as they were never meant to go into a book for knitters. They came about for different reasons.

I wanted 'Tropical Fish' and did my fishing from Lee's Mac screen saver as they swam past. The '1920's Golf' was designed for the Museum Collection catalogue. 'Sunset at Sea' was one Lee wanted for herself and she knitted the original. 'Fabiola Lily' was designed for a friend, and 'Energy' for the gallery for fall 94/95. The other cotton garments (Landscape Vest, Country Garden Vest and Watercolour Squares) and all the Galway and Encore garments were designed, knitted and photographed from scratch... like pancakes.

When you are knitting them remember that they are your sweaters. You can adapt them to your ability level by adding or leaving out some of the images — we promise not to send the knitting inspector in the middle of the night. If you do get into a terrrrible tangle, just lay your knitting down, eat chocolate and drink champagne until you feel you can handle it again.

Lee and I hope you enjoy this book as much as we enjoyed creating it.

Contents

This book and all yarns in this book are available through
The Plymouth Yarn Company, Inc.
P.O Box 28, 500 Lafayette Street, Bristol, Pennsylvania 19007, USA
Phone: (215) 788-0459

Published 1994
Vibrant Handknits, USA, Inc.
for The Plymouth Yarn Company
P.O. Box 28, Briston, PA 19007, USA
Copyright © Lee Andersen

Tropical Fish

Each fish is a little work of art in this view of the world under the sea. Colourful fish breathe precious pearl bubbles and float among painterly seaweed in multicoloured yarns. Embroidered fins in metallic threads add shimmer to take this beautiful sweater from day into night.

Plymouth Yarns Required

All COTTON SOFT (50 gm balls)
(A) #263 navy x 16 (17,18)
(C) #060 jade x 1
(D) #269 blue green x 1
(G) #247 cerulean blue x 20 yds
(H) #899 black x 14 yds
(I) #800 white x 8 yds
(J) #709 yellow x 7 yds
(K) #361 red x 8 yds
(L) #339 orange x 1
(M) seahorse embroidered heavily with yellow (J)
(N) #319 hot pink x 1
(P) #616 dark cerise x 6 yds
(Q) #628 purple x 4 yds
(R) black and white together x 10 yds
(U) #631 blue x 1
(V) #9001 blue lilac for seaweed embroidery x 8 yds

FINISHING TOUCHES
Pink metallic x 8 yds
Red metallic thread x 3 yds
Silver chainette x 30 yds
Gold chainette x 30 yds
35 to 40 4 mm pearls

Photocopy colour list and attach a small strand of each colour before taking paper bands off the balls.

Needles
Bands: 3¹/₂ mm (U.S. #4, U.K. #9 or #10)
Circular needles as above
Body: 4¹/₂ mm (U.S. #7, U.K. #7) or as required to achieve the following tension:

Tension or Gauge
20 sts to 4" or 10 cm
28 rows to 4" or 10 cm

Garment Size
Width: 100 (110, 120) sts = 20" or 51 cm (22" or 56 cm, 24" or 61 cm)
Length: 26¹/₂" or 67 cm

Back
Using navy and band needles, cast on 90 (100, 110) sts. Rib (K1, P1) for 24 rows.
Change to body needles and increase evenly to 100 (110, 120) sts. Work graph beginning on the bottom right corner front facing.

Alternatively choose any favorite fish from the front and place as desired. Begin back neck shaping 5 rows from end. Place centre 12 sts on holder. Work 2 tog each row 5 times. Cast off shoulders.

Front
As back but shape the neck 24 rows from the end. Put the central 12 sts on a holder and decrease as graph till 39 (44, 49) sts remain on each shoulder. Continue straight for remainder of graph. Cast off loosely.

Sleeves
Using the band needles and navy cast on 40 sts and rib for 24 rows. Increase to 56 sts, change to body needles and begin the graph. Increase one each side every 6th row till until desired length. Cast off loosely. Do other sleeve using second graph.

Neckband
Sew shoulder seams. Using navy and the circular needles pick up and knit 92 sts as follows: 30 sts down one front, 10 from the holder, 30 from other side of front and then knit up 22 across the back of the neck. Rib for 24 rows and cast off loosely in knit. Fold outwards and sew down each stitch allowing the neck to remain elastic.

Finishing
Embroider as shown on graph. Sew the sleeve seams. Sew from the right side and work up through the bar on either side alternatively.

Sew the side seams up to the armhole. (9" from shoulder). Stretch the sleeve slightly and set the sleeve into the armhole using the kitchener method of working behind a complete stitch on the sleeve and then up through the bar on the body. Skip every third row on the body.

Embroidery
Work satin stitch embroidery over and over on the yellow seahorse to make his tummy fat.

Make seaweed by laying variegated yarn along lines as shown on graph. Couch or stitch in position.

Add metallic fins, gills and tails to fish. Add bubbles by working metallic thread over and over one stitch or sew on pearls.

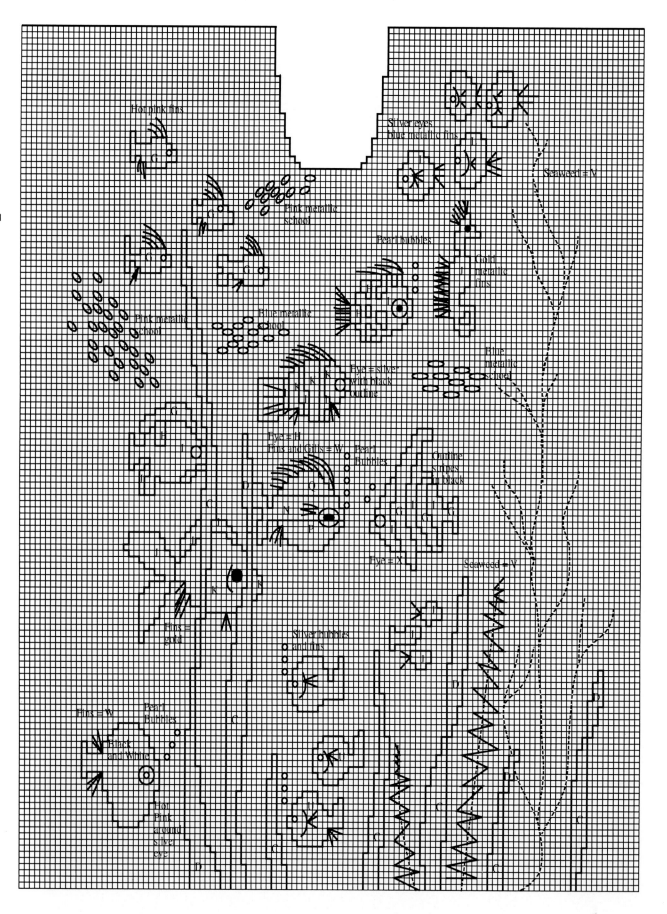

Hot pink fins

Silver eyes
blue metallic fins

Seaweed ≡ lv

Pink metallic
school

Pearl bubbles

Gold
metallic
fins

Pink metallic
school

Blue metallic
school

Blue
metallic
school

Eye ≡ silver
with black
outline

Eye ≡ lt
Fins and Gills ≡ lv

Pearl
Bubbles

Outline
stripes
in black

Eye ≡ lx

Seaweed ≡ lv

Fins ≡
gold

Silver bubbles
and fins

Fins ≡ lv

Pearl
Bubbles

Black
and white

Hot
Pink
around
Silver
eye

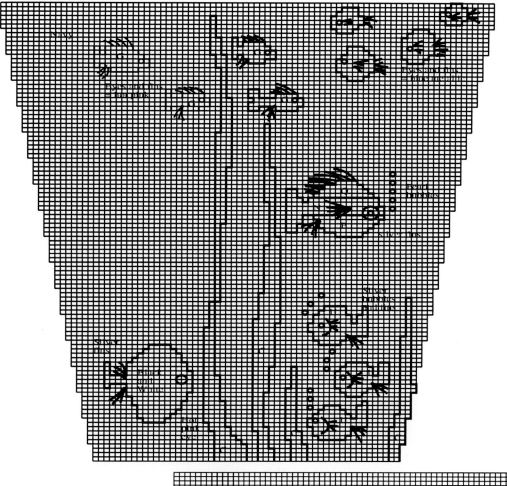

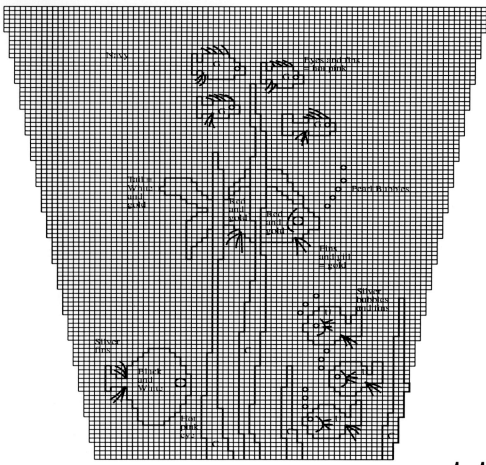

Watercolour Squares

This simple design is a joy to knit and easy for him to wear. The colour changing yarn is worked in squares in random positions. Place them where ever you wish. Each square uses exactly one yard of yarn. Cut these before beginning and keep them at hand for when the urge strikes. There is no wrong place to put them.

Plymouth Yarns Required
(50 gm balls)
(A) COTTON SOFT #899 black
     x 16 (17,18)
(B) COTTON SOFT #9941
     denim - gray x 1

Needles
$3^1/_2$ mm (U.S. #5, U.K. #9)
for bands
Circular needles as above for
the neckband
$4^1/_2$ mm (U.S. #7, U.K. #7)
for body

Garment Size
Width: 100 (110, 120) sts = 20" or
50 cm (22" or 56 cm, 24" or 61 cm)
Length: 170 rows of body plus
bands = 27" or 69 cm
Sleeve = $20^1/_2$" or 55 cm or as
desired

Tension or Gauge
20 sts to 4" or 10 cm
28 rows to 4" or 10 cm

Back
Using body needles and (A) cast
on 90 (100, 110) sts. Rib for 3".
(K 1, P 1 across row.)
Repeat this row till band
measures 3". On a back facing
row using purl, increase to 100
(110, 120) sts. Change to stocking
stitch (knit front facing rows and
purl back facing rows.) Each
coloured square is 5 sts and 6
rows. Carry the black yarn
behind the coloured squares.
Cross yarns every stitch rather

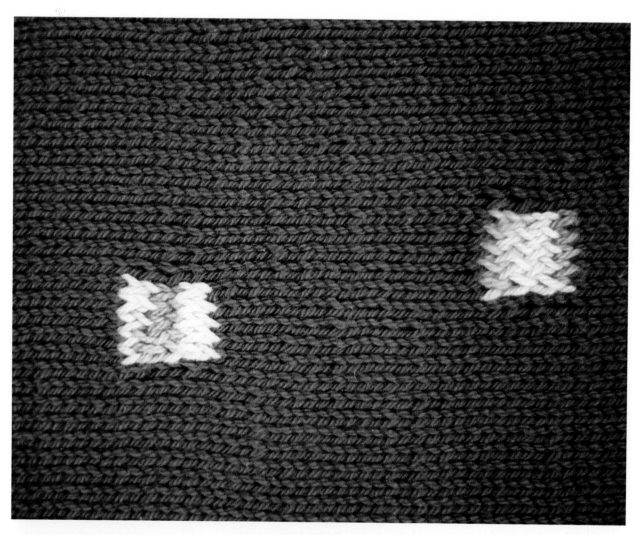

than carrying straight across all five sts. This creates the woven look. Work about 25 squares randomly on the back.

Work the back neck as follows: Put the central 20 sts on a holder and work two sts together at neck edges every row five times until 35 (40, 45) sts remain. Cast off. Work other shoulder to match.

Front
Work as back but place the squares in different positions. When 30 rows remain put the central 20 sts on a holder. Complete row. Work two sts together at neck edges each front facing row five times until 35 (40, 45) sts remain. Continue straight

until 30 rows have been worked from beginning of front neck shaping. Cast off. Work other shoulder to match.

Sleeves
Cast on 43 (47, 49) sts using black and work ribbing as for bands. Change to body needles and increase to 52 (54, 56) sts. Increase one each edge every 4th row until sleeve measures 20" or

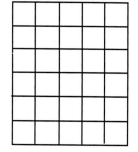

required length. Work about 11 squares on each sleeve. Cast off loosely. Sew shoulder seams.

Neckband
Using the circular needles, black and the right side facing, pick up and knit 20 sts down the side of the front neck, 20 sts from the centre front , 20 sts from the remaining front diagonal and then 30 sts from the back of the neck. (90 sts). Rib for 20 rows. Cast off loosely. Fold the neck inside and stitch down.

Finishing
Work in all tails. Press gently from the wrong side. Sew the side seams and arm seams neatly. Set sleeves deeply. Sew remaining tails.

Floral Encore

This English garden cardigan in the style of a Jacobean tapestry is both charming and practical. The bands, cuffs, pockets and fold back collar are edged in an easy to knit decorative stitch in four colours. Although this garment has all the richness of a classic wool garment is has the added advantage of being knitted in Plymouth Encore —a machine washable yarn.

Plymouth Yarns Required
(100 gm balls)
(A) ENCORE #473 teal mix x 4
(B) ENCORE #354 blueberry mix x 1
(C) ENCORE #385 turquoise mix x 1
(D) ENCORE #044 blue thunder x 1
(E) ENCORE #504 eggplant x 1
(F) ENCORE #217 black x 1
(G) ENCORE #213 caribe green x 1
(H) ENCORE #180 dark mauve x 1
(I) ENCORE #223 brown x 1
(J) ENCORE #355 garnett mix x 1

Needles
3¹/₂ mm (U.S. #4, U.K. #9 or #10) for the bands.
4¹/₂ mm (U.S. #7, U.K. #7) for the body

5 buttons

Tension or Gauge
20 sts to 4" or 10 cm
26 rows to 4" or 10 cm

Garment Size
Width: 120 sts = 24" or 61 cm
Length: 150 rows of graph = 23 plus 2" band = 25" or 63 cm

Back
Using band needles and (A) "teal mix" cast on (110) sts.
Work band pattern as follows:
Row 1, 2, 3 and 4: *K1, P1* repeat between * and * to end.
Row 5 to 8: *P1, K1 using (B) "blueberry mix"
Row 9 to 12: *K1, P1* using (E) "eggplant"
Row 13 to 16: *P1, K1* using (J) "garnett"

On the next purl row increase to (120) sts. Change to body needles and stocking stitch (Knit the front facing rows and purl the back facing rows.) Tie on (A). Begin graph.

Continue working until 5 rows from the end. Put the central 20 sts on a holder. Work 2 tog at the neck edges on every row 5 times. Cast off 45 shoulder sts. Work other shoulder to match.

Left Front (while facing)
Cast on 50 sts in (A). Work bottom band to match back. Increase to 57 sts. Use RIGHT side of graph (NOT LEFT as expected) for 30 rows.

Pocket Band
On row 31 work 18 sts, KNIT 20 sts in (A) to establish pocket band position. Return to graph for remainder of row.

Continue as graph except on the 20 sts of pocket band. Work pocket band at same time and in band pattern but using only 2 rows of each colour (8 rows total).

After the 8 rows have been worked, cast off 20 pocket band stitches. Put all other sts on holding thread.

Pocket Lining
At inside top of bottom band using (F) pick up the 20 sts below the cast off pocket band. Stocking stitch for 26 rows. Work the 8 rows of graph which the pocket band replaced. Put all sts (57) back on needles and continue graph.

Neck Shaping
Work neck shaping as follows: at 70 rows of graph work 2 tog at neck edge of each front facing row till 46 remain.

Continue straight till end of graph. Cast off.

Right Front (while facing)
Work other front using the 57 sts of the LEFT side of graph. Begin pocket band on row 31 as follows: Knit 18 sts, knit 20 in (A) to establish pocket, knit 19 from graph. Work as for other pocket.

Continue on graph until neck shaping begins at row 70. Reverse shaping from other front.

Continue straight until end of graph. Cast off.

Sleeves
Cast on 34 sts using band needles. Work bottom band pattern.

Change to body needles and increase to 50 sts.

Begin graph on row 71. Increase one each edge every 6th row thereafter until graph is completed (80 rows). On next front facing row begin brown and black diamond working first stitch on stitch number 20.

Complete diamond and work 5 more rows in background yarn.

For more length work in background yarn and add any other image from the graph as desired. Cast off loosely.

Make second sleeve using same graph — do not reverse pattern.

Sew shoulder seams.

Front Band and Collar
The front buttonband and collar is all worked in one, beginning at the back of the neck. Put sts from back of neck onto band needle.

Tie on yarn (A). Pick up and work all new sts knitwise when facing the front and purlwise when facing the back. Pick up 5 sts from the diagonal (to the shoulder seam) at the back of the neck.

Turn, rib those 5 sts and the sts from the back of the neck. Pick up 5 more sts from other diagonal (to shoulder seam). Turn, rib back

Continue in this fashion picking up 15 new sts (one from each row) at the end of each ribbed row until reaching the first decrease on the neck shaping on the front. Cut (A).

Retie at beginning of bottom band. Knit up sts along remaining front. Knit up every stitch from edge of bottom band and skip every 3rd stitch along stocking stitch = 62 sts. Rib the collar sts and then pick up 62 sts down the remaining front.

Change the ribbing pattern to begin the first step of the band pattern. Work 2 rows in (A). Continue the band pattern in (B) for 2 rows.

Button Hole Row
On first row of (E) work the first buttonhole (yarn over, knit 2 tog) at the corner. Work band pattern for 10 sts and work next buttonhole. The 5th buttonhole should be at top of bottom band. Work band pattern to end of row. Work one more row in (E) and then two rows in (J). Cast off firmly on 3rd row of (J).

Finishing
Sew side seams and sleeve seams. Sew sides of pockets to insides of fronts. Set sleeves in deeply. Sew in tails. Press gently. Add buttons.

Top

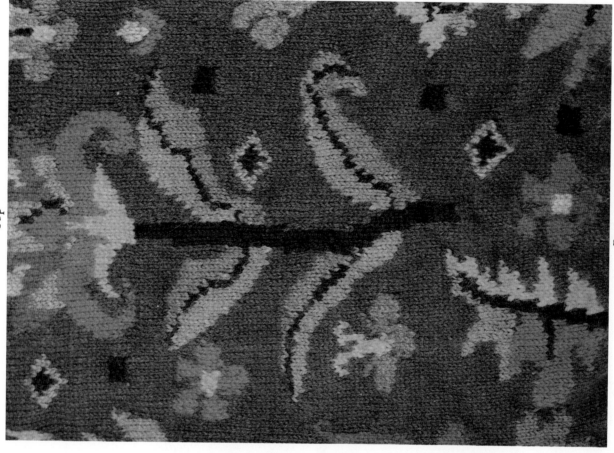

Bottom

Spare Yarn

This design requires lots of
background yarn and only smal
amounts of the accent colours.
The colours of the left over yarn
all work together well.

Try making a smaller child's
version of the cardigan but
change the background colour.

Use any single image or any
combination of images from
the graph.

For a boys cardigan or pullover
use the copper brown as the
background and make the
diamonds in black and blue.

Contentment Coat

Simple blocks of pretty colours combine in this warm oversize cardigan in machine washable Encore used double throughout. Use large needle sizes for a casual oversized cardigan look, or smaller needles for a firmer, more formal jacket look.

Plymouth Yarns Required
(100 gm balls)
(A) ENCORE #473 teal mix x 4
(B) ENCORE #180 dark mauve x 1
(C) ENCORE #213 caribe green x 2
(D) ENCORE #044 blue thunder x 1
(E) ENCORE #355 garnett mix x 2
(F) ENCORE #433 mauve mix x 1
(G) ENCORE #354 blueberry mix x 2
(H) ENCORE #504 eggplant x 2
(I) ENCORE #194 grey heather x 1

8 buttons

Needles
4 mm (U.S. #6, U.K. #8 or #9)
for the bands
5.5 mm (U.S. #10, U.K. #5 or #4)
for the body or required size to
achieve gauge.

Tension or Gauge
13 sts to 4" or 10 cm
18 rows to 4" or 10 cm

Garment Size
Width = 90 sts = 27^1/$_2$" or 70 cm
Length = 120 rows of graph plus
3" band = 29" or 74 cm

Back
Using band needles and (A)
DOUBLED cast on 80 sts.
Rib 15 rows or 3".
(K1, P1 across row).
On the next wrong side facing
row, increase in purl 10 sts to 90

sts. Change to body needles and stocking stitch (knit the front facing rows and purl the back facing rows.)

On a front facing row begin the graph. Continue straight until back neck shaping (5 rows from end). Put the central 12 sts on a holder. Work 2 tog at the neck edge every row 5 times. Cast off remaining 34 sts for shoulder. Work other shoulder to match.

Front

Work front body and band at the same time.

Cast on 44 sts in (A) using band needles. Rib 3".

On next wrong side facing row, increase as follows: Work band rib for 8 sts, purl the rest of the row increasing 4 sts evenly across the row (8 front band pattern, 40 graph sts = 48 sts).

Change to body needles. Work the outside 40 sts of the graph in stocking stitch while maintaining the band pattern as established and in (A). Use a stitch marker to maintain the division between the band pattern and body.

Since ribbing is longer than stocking stitch, MISS every 9th and 10 row of the ribbed front band while still working the graph. This will make the band 20 rows less than the body and the correct gauge to match the stocking stitch body.

Pocket Edging

After 30 rows work the outside 4 sts in ribbing for 20 rows to form the pocket edging at side seam. Continue straight till 25 rows from the end.

Neckhole

Put the 8 band pattern sts and 4 body sts on a holder. Next row:

work two together at the neck edge each front facing row until 34 sts remain. Continue straight until front matches the back. Cast off.

Front with Buttonhole Band

Reverse instructions for other front but also add buttonholes as follows:

on row 3 of bottom band, and then on row 3 of graph work a buttonhole. Stitch 4 should be a purl stitch. K1, P1, K1, yarn to front (this will form a yarn over), K2 together, P1, K1, P1.

Work further buttonholes every 12th row thereafter of button band (not graph). Work the final buttonhole on the pick up row of the collar making 8 buttonholes including the one in the collar.

Sleeve

Work both sleeves the same. Using band needles and (A) cast on 38 sts. Rib for 3". Change to body needles and increase to 46 sts. Use centre of back graph but change G to H. Increase one each edge every 4th row while working the graph up to 62 sts. Continue straight for 70 rows of graph (or desired length). Cast off loosely. Set sleeve deeply into armhole.

Collar

Sew shoulder seams. Use band needles and work firmly. Pick up 12 sts along back of neck in (A). Rib back. Pick up 3 stitches at the end of every row in stocking stitch regardless of the ribbed pattern. On the following row work the new stitches as normal ribbing. When you reach the button band pick up all band sts on same row and make button-hole in centre of band on same row.

When all sts are picked up (94 sts in 22 rows) work 10 more rows

and then cast off all button band and buttonhole band sts on the next two rows. Continue casting off 3 sts at the beginning of each row until 30 remain. Cast off final 30.

Fold in half and stitch in place. Do not cover the buttonhole formed on the pick up row.

Pocket Linings

Sew side seams leaving the pocket edging open. Cast on 20 st in any remaining yarn and st st for 30 rows. Cast off. Sew cast off row of pocket to inside front, in line with the top of the pocket edging. Sew side of pocket to side seam of back. Sew remaining two sides to inside front with the bottom of the pocket 10 rows below the pocket edging.

Finishing

Sew in remaining tails. Press gently. Sew on 8 buttons.

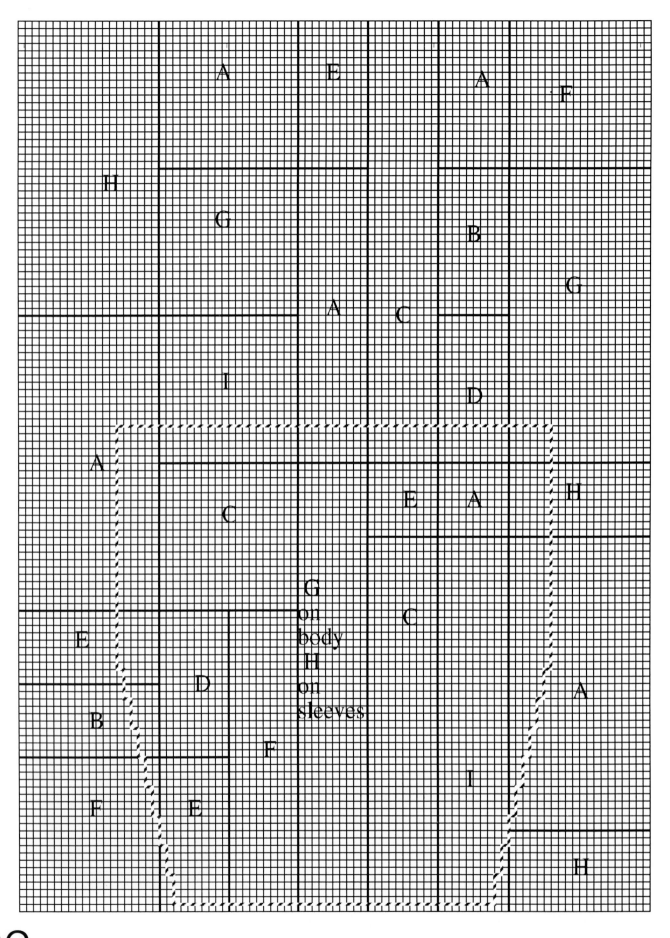

1920's Golf

This charming picture of golfers from an earlier time uses Plymouth Cotton Soft cotton, intarsia and some basic embroidery. The pocket on her sweater is three dimensional and the little golf ball is attached later.

Plymouth Yarns Required

All COTTON SOFT (50 gm balls)
(A) #032 blue green
    for bottom x 9 (10, 11)
(B) #034 blue for sky x 3 (3, 3)
(C) #062 green for trees x4 (4, 4)
(D) #899 black x 1
(E) #800 white x 5 yds
(F) #616 red pink x 1
(G) #631 water blue x 1
(H) #628 purple x 1
(I) #709 gold x 1
(J) #843 grey x 1
(K) #536 green for embroidery
    trees x 1
(L) #361 sweater embroidery x 5 yds

Needles

$3^{1}/_{2}$ mm (U.S. #4, U.K. #9 or #10)
for the bands
Circular needle of the same size
for the neck bands
4 or $4^{1}/_{2}$ mm (U.S. #6 or #7,
U.K. #7 or #8) for the body

Tension or Gauge

20 sts to 10 cm or 4"
27 rows to 10 cm or 4"

Garment Size

Width: 100 (110, 120) sts = 20" or
50 cm (22" or 56 cm, 24" or 61) cm
Length: 160 rows of graph plus 3"
band = $26^{1}/_{2}$" or 67 cm

Back

Using band needles and (A)
cast on 90 (100, 110) sts. Rib
(K1, P1 across row every row)
for 21 rows.   On the next purl
row increase 10 sts to 120 sts
and change to body needles and
stocking stitch (knit the front
facing rows and purl the back

facing rows.) Begin graph but
leave off the two golfers.

Back Neck Shaping.

Put the central 20 sts on a
holder. Work 2 tog at the neck
edge on each row until 5 sts
have been used. Cast off
shoulder. Work other shoulder
to match.

Front

As back until graph. Add the
two golfers. Work pocket on

female golfer's sweater as
follows: Do the 4 sts and 5 rows
of pocket in (L). Cast off the 4
pocket sts. Go back to the
beginning of the pocket on the
inside. Work these same sts and
rows in (F). Then begin working
with all the sts again using
graph.

Continue until 25 rows from the
end. Put the 16 central stitches
on a holder. Work two together
at the neck edge each front facing

row seven times. Continue straight until front matches the back.

Sleeve

Cast on 48 sts using black and work ribbing as for bands. Change to body needles and increase to 56 sts. Increase one each edge on the 6th rows until sleeve is long enough. Cast off loosely.

Neckband

Sew shoulder seams.
Pick up 90 sts around neck hole one for each complete stitch and rib 21 rows in bottom colour. Cast off, sew seam and fold in and stitch down.

Embroidery

Use chain stitch to make swirls on trees in (K). Stitch mouth on female golfer using (L). Add lines to define arm and ribbed sweater pattern on her sweater in (L).

Split black yarn. Lay down and couch lines on argyle vest in black. Make tiny golf ball using needle embroidery or fine crochet and attach as shown.

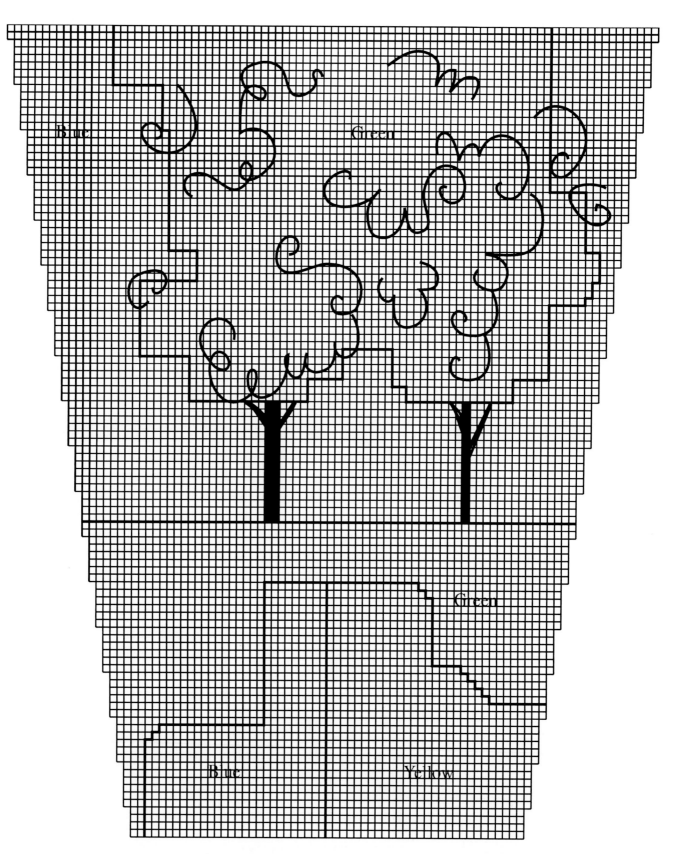

Bold and Brilliant

This sharp classic is easy to knit with eight exciting colours.

Plymouth Yarns Required
(100 gm hanks)
(A) GALWAY #22 turquoise x 1
(B) GALWAY #16 red x 1
(C) GALWAY #24 purple x 1
(D) GALWAY #45 green x 2 (2, 2)
(E) GALWAY #9 black x 1
(F) GALWAY #11 blue x 1
(G) GALWAY #23 hot pink x 1
(H) GALWAY #18 dark teal x 1

Needles
4 mm (U.S. #6, U.K. #8) for bands and circular needle for the neckband
4¹/₂mm (U.S. #7, U.K. #7) for body

Tension or Gauge
20 sts and 27 rows to 4" or 10 cm
Width: 100 sts = 20" (110 sts = 22", 120 sts = 24")
Length with bands: 25"

Front
Using body needles and (E) cast on in black 90 (100, 110) sts.
Rib in black for 3".
On a back facing row using purl increase to 100 (110, 120) sts.

Change to stocking stitch (knit front facing row and purl back facing rows) and begin graph.

Shape neck as follows: 20 rows from end put central 20 sts on holder. K2 tog at neck edges on front facing rows 5 times then work straight for 10 rows. Cast off remaining 30 (40, 45) sts for each shoulder.

Back:
Work ribbed band as front.
Increase for body. Cut black.

Tie on red work 55 sts. Tie on blue work 55 sts to end. Work as established for 72 rows.

Change red to purple and blue to teal. After 24 rows of purple change purple to magenta pink. Continue until 43 rows of pink have been worked.

Put the central 20 sts on a holder. Complete row. Work two sts together at each neck edge each row five times till 35 (40, 45) sts remain. Cast off. Work other shoulder to match.

Left Sleeve

Cast on 43 (47, 49) sts using black for each cuff. Rib as for bottom band. Increase to 53 (55, 57) sts. Tie on turquoise. Increase one each edge every 6th row. Change to green at row 33.
When sleeve is desired length cast off loosely.

Right Sleeve

As left sleeve but begin with green and end with turquoise.

Neckband

Sew shoulder seams.

Using the neck band needles, black and the right side facing, pick up and knit 19 sts down the side of the front neck, 20 sts from the centre front ,19 sts from the remaining front diagonal and 30 sts from the back of the neck. Rib for 24 rows. Cast off loosely in knit. Fold the neck outside and stitch down.

Finishing

Work in all tails. Press gently from the wrong side. Sew the side seams and arm seams neatly. Sew armhole seams.

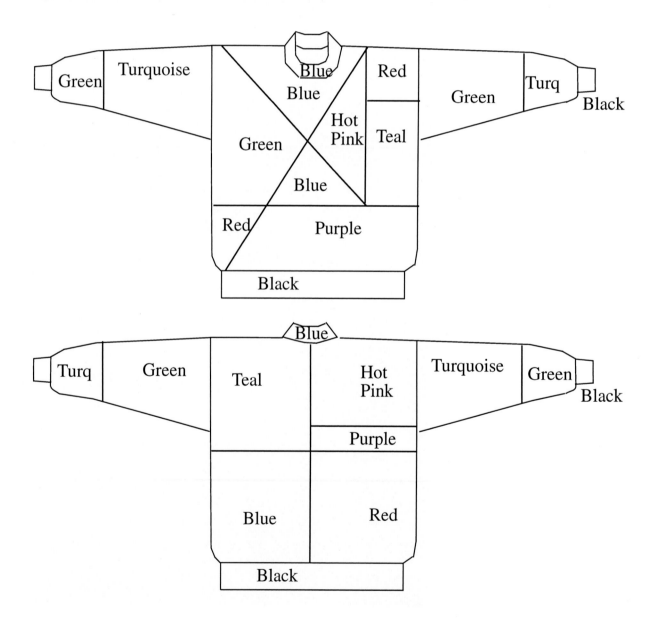

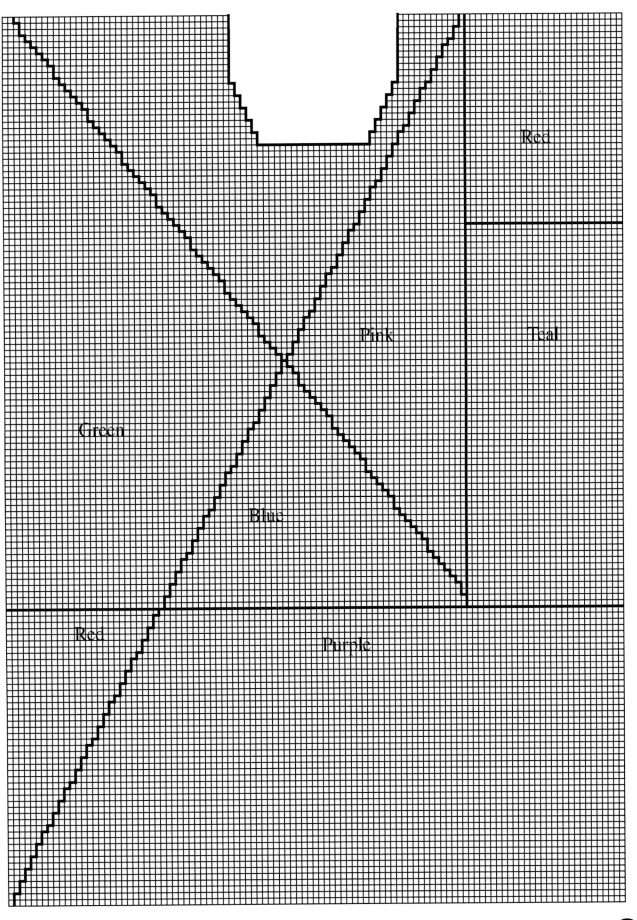

Race Winner

In the beginning of language, white and black were the first two colors named: lightness and darkness. A square was one of the first geometric shapes named. The combination is power and simplicity itself.

Plymouth Yarns Required
(100 gm hanks)
(A) GALWAY #09 black x 5
(B) GALWAY 8 white x 4
(C) GALWAY #23 magenta x 1
(D) GALWAY #45 green x 1
(E) GALWAY #16 red x 1

Needles
4¹/₂ mm (U.S. #7, U.K. #7)
for the bands and body

Tension or Gauge
20 sts to 4" or 10 cm
27 rows to 4" or 10 cm

Garment Size
Width: 110 sts = 22" or 56 cm
Length: 28" or 71 cm or as
desired

Back
Cast on 110 sts using body needles and black. Stocking stitch (knit the front facing rows and purl the back facing rows) as follows.

Row 1: (front facing row) K70 black, tie on white, K40 white.
Row 2: (back facing row) P40 white, P70 black.

Continue as established until 100 stocking stitch rows have been worked.

Row 101: (front facing row) K70 white, K40 black.
Continue as established until 5 rows from end.

Back Neck Shaping
Put the central 20 sts on a holder. Work 2 tog at the neck edge on each row 5 times. Cast off remaining 40 sts. Work other shoulder to match.

Front
As back until 25 rows from the end. Put the 20 central stitches on a holder. Work two together at the neck edge each front facing row five times. Continue straight until front matches the back.

Sleeve
Cast on 60 sts in black using body needles. Work pattern as follows:
10 black, 10 white. Do not carry behind. Use separate 5 yds lengths.

Change order every 14 rows to make checkerboard effect. Increase one each edge every

6th row until sleeve is desired length. Cast off loosely at a natural break.

Bands
Work separately on a diagonal and attach later.
Using band needles cast on 1 stitch in magenta.

Make 3 sts from that one stitch. Purl back increasing one stitch at the beginning of this and every purl row until band is long enough to go around whole body.

Tie on red. *Cast on 2 sts at the beginning of the row and cast on one at the beginning of the next purl row.* Repeat from * to * (9 sts).

Carry magenta up from rows below. Work as for red (15 sts) Knit the next front facing row in green and knit the next wrong side facing row in green. Repeat from first * till 20 sts have accumulated.

Continue in colour pattern as established. Continue increasing one on the beginning of every purl row but now work two together at the beginning of every knit row.

Work as established until band is long enough to fit around whole body. Maintain the decreases on the front facing row but also begin decreasing 2 on each wrong side facing row until no sts remain.

Finishing
Although the bands may be attached using hand sewing techniques it is easier to use a sewing machine. Join the two ends. One edge is more elastic. Machine sew this edge to the body. Fold band in half. Hand

stitch remaining edge to body.

Work cuffs and neckband using same concept adjusting length as desired.

Flowers
Swiss darn or duplicate stitch flowers using chart. Work main flower in red. Work two flowers on either side in magenta. Chain stitch the leaves under each flower and stalks in green.

Option
If you prefer a more traditional look, rib the bands and cuffs. An additional hank of black or white will be needed.

Bottom Bands
Use a smaller size needle 4 mm (U.S. #5, U.K. # 8). Cast on 100 sts. Rib for 3". Purl next wrong side facing row evenly increasing 10 stitches across the row.

Continue with pattern given.

Cuffs
As for bottom bands but cast on 48 sts and increase to 60 sts.

Neck Band
With smaller needles pick up and knit 90 sts around neck opening. Rib for 24 rows. Cast off loosely. Fold to inside and stitch down.

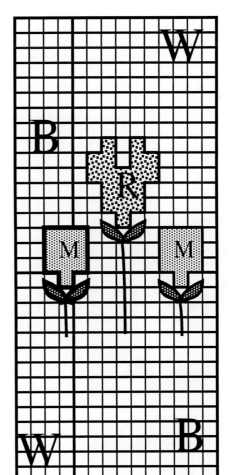

Green stalks and leaves

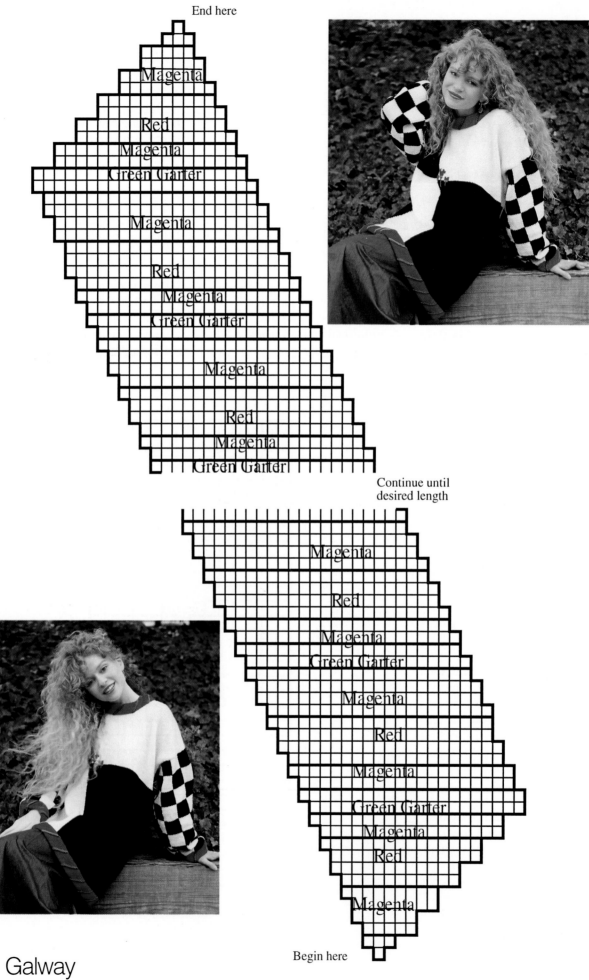

End here

Magenta

Red
Magenta
Green Garter

Magenta

Red
Magenta
Green Garter

Magenta

Red
Magenta
Green Garter

Continue until
desired length

Magenta

Red

Magenta
Green Garter

Magenta

Red

Magenta

Green Garter
Magenta
Red

Magenta

Begin here

Shades of Jade Argyle

This sharp classic unisex sweater is easy to knit and easy for him or her to wear.

Plymouth Yarns Required

(100 gm hanks)
(A) GALWAY #22 turquoise x 1
(B) GALWAY #9 black x 2
(C) GALWAY #18 dark
      teal x 5 (6, 6)
(D) GALWAY #24 purple x 1

Needles

4 mm (U.S. #5, U.K. #9) straight for bands and circular for neckband
4¹/₂ mm (U.S. #7, U.K. #7) for body

Tension or Gauge

20 sts to 4" or 10 cm
26 rows to 4" or 10 cm

Garment Size

Width: 100 (110, 120) sts
20" or 50 cm (22" or 56 cm, 24" or 59 cm
Length: 170 graph rows = 27" or 69 cm

Back

Using band needles and (A) cast on in black 91 (101, 111) sts.
Fairisle rib in teal and black for 3" as follows:
Row 1: Knit 1 black , Purl 1 teal across row.
Row 2: K 1 teal , P 1 black across row.
Repeat these 2 rows till 18 rows have been worked. With teal purl on a back facing row and increase to 100 (110, 120) sts.
Change to stocking stitch (knit front facing rows and purl back facing rows) and body needles. Begin graph.

Black Vee

All black is worked in a simple ribbed pattern which changes every 4th row. When the graph widens work those sts in black and in knit on the front facing rows. Wind the black into two balls. Make sure the first row of the graph is a front facing knit row so all purl rows are simply a repeat of the row below.

Row 1: RSF (Right Side Facing) Work the central stitch of the graph in black.
Row 2: Purl across row matching colours.
Row 3: As row 1.
Row 4: As row 2.
Row 5: RSF. To extend the triangle and change the ribbed pattern - knit the stitch either side of the centre black stitch in black and purl the centre stitch.
Row 6: in new pattern as established.
Row 9: RSF. To extend the triangle and change the ribbed pattern - knit the stitch either side of the black stitches in black and purl the next stitch and knit the centre stitch.

Continue as established until the black triangle in the middle is 7 sts wide. On the next front facing row work 4 sts in black as established. Work the central stitch in purple stocking stitch. Tie on a new ball of black and work 4 more stitches in black. Continue as established and make a purple vee in the centre in stocking stitch while maintaining the black patterned vee.

Work the fine black lines inside the argyle in purple and then swiss darn over them later in black. Continue using the graph until the second argyle graph has been completed. Work 5 (10, 14) rows. Work the back neck as follows: Put the central 20 sts

on a holder and work two sts together at each neck edge each row five times till 35 (40, 45) sts remain. Cast off. Work other shoulder to match.

Front

Work as for back until 30 rows remain. (Or 7 black stitches remain on the last argyle graph.) Next front facing row work the next row of the argyle (5 black sts remain) work 11 in teal. Put the central 20 sts on a holder. Complete row. K2 tog at each neck edge each front facing row five times until 35 (40, 45) sts remain. Continue straight until 30 rows have been worked from beginning of front neck shaping. Cast off. Work other shoulder to match.

Sleeves

Cast on 43 (47, 49) sts using black and work fairisle ribbing as for bands. Change to body needles and increase to 53 (55, 57) sts. Increase one each edge on the 4th row. Begin argyle graph on 5th row and centre stitch. Continue until argyle is

completed. Work one row in black stocking stitch then work the fairisle rib for 8 rows. Cast off loosely.

Neckband

Sew shoulder seams. Using the neck band needles, (C) and the right side facing, pick up and knit 20 sts down the side of the front neck, 21 sts from the centre front , 20 sts from the remaining front diagonal and then the 31 sts from the back of the neck. (92 sts) Work the fairisle rib for 24 rows. Cast off loosely. Fold the neck inside and stitch down or leave high as desired.

Embroidery

Using an embroidery needle work in swiss darning or duplicate stitch over the top of the knitted stitches in black to form the dividing lines inside the argyle.

Finishing

Work in all tails. Press gently from the wrong side. Sew the side seams and arm seams neatly. Sew armhole seams.

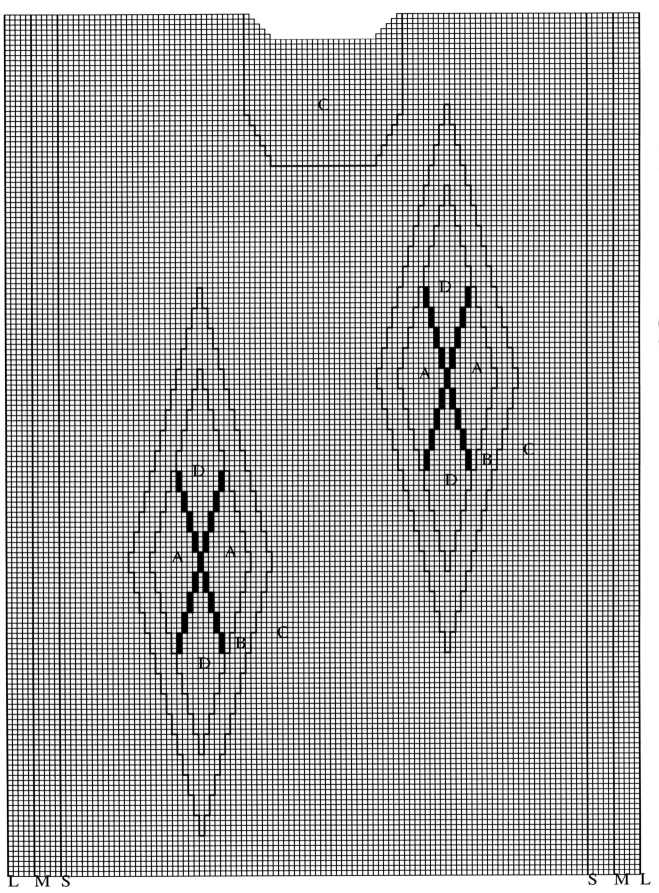

Valley Flowers

This flattering and feminine pattern has a deep vee filled with mint leaves and three dimensional flowers made of Plymouth Cotton Soft yarn. Cables accent the cuffs, bands and neck band. Instructions for a tunic for a fuller figure are included.

Plymouth Yarns Required

(A) GALWAY #704 charcoal
   100 gm hank x 5
(B) GALWAY #9 black
   100 gm hanks x 1
(C) GALWAY #8 white
   100 gm hank x 1
(D) CLECKHEATON MOHAIR
   12 ply #210 green x 30 yds
   for leaves
(E) COTTON SOFT #9001 blue lilac
   x 1 for flowers

Needles

4 mm (U.S. #6, U.K. #8) for bands
Circular needle of same size for the neckband
Cable needle of same size
4¹/₂mm (U.S. #7, U.K. #7) for body, or size needed to achieve tension as follows
Crochet hook for flowers 3.5 mm

Tension or Gauge

20 sts to 4" or 10 cm
26 rows to 4" or 10

Size

Width: 101 sts = 19¹/₂" or 50 cm
Length with bands: 140 graph rows plus 3" bands = 30" or 77 cm

Tunic

This pattern and design is ideal for the fuller figure. Cast on using the body sts and body needles. To add 2" extra width add 5 sts to each side using the charcoal.

To make the tunic 60" around (30" width) add 27 sts to each side of the graph.

Remember the sleeves will need to be shortened by 1" for every

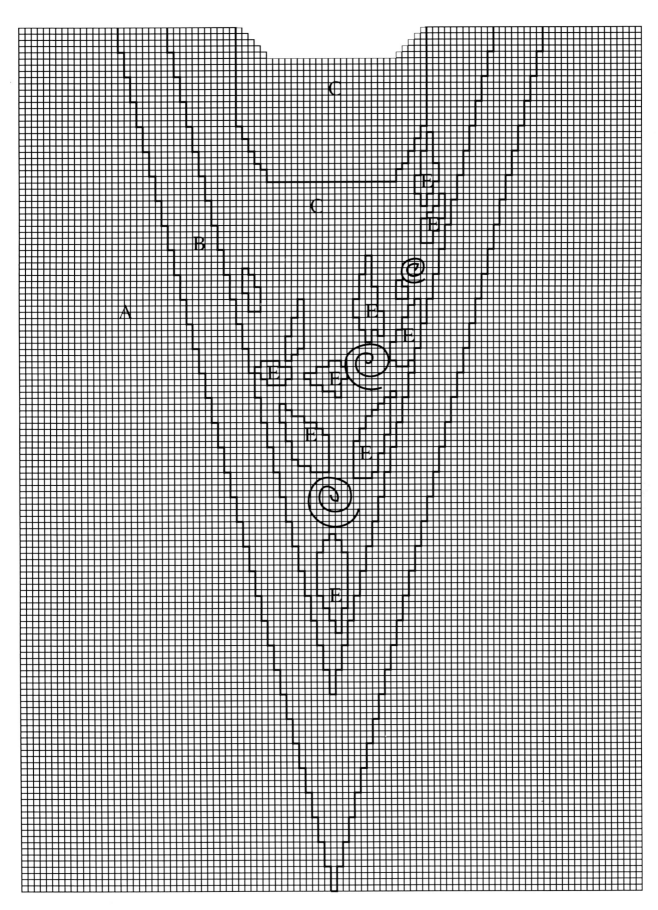

inch added to the body width.

Back

Using band needles for the pullover or body needles for the tunic, and (A) cast on 91 (ideally any number divisible by 7 for the tunic) sts.

Row 1: Knit 4, Purl 3 across row.
Row 2: K3, P4
Row 3: Cable row (front facing row) Place the first 2 knit sts onto the cable needle, hold in back, knit next 2 sts, knit 2 sts from cable needle, purl 3. Repeat across row.
Row 4: as row 2

Repeat these four rows until the band is 3" long. On a back facing row using purl increase to 101 sts (or as desired - add or decrease one to make an odd number so the centre vee begins with a single stitch.)

Change to body needles and stocking stitch (knit front facing row and purl back facing rows.)

Begin graph immediately for the length as shown. For a longer tunic work any number of rows in (A) to add length before beginning the graph. Add 26 rows for an extra 4" or 10 cm.

Black Vee

Wind the black into two balls. All black is worked in a simple ribbed pattern which changes every 4th row. When the vee widens work the outside sts in black and in knit on the front facing rows.

Work the first graph row as a front facing knit row so all purl rows are simply a repeat of the row below.

Row 1: RSF (Right Side Facing) Work the central stitch of the graph in black as a purl stitch.

Row 2: Purl across row matching colours.

Row 3: As row 1
Row 4: As row 2

Row 5: RSF. To extend the triangle and change the ribbed pattern - knit the stitch either side of the centre black stitch in black and purl the centre stitch.

Row 6: in new pattern as established.

Row 9: RSF. To extend the triangle and change the ribbed pattern - knit the stitch either side of the black stitches in black and purl the next stitch and knit the centre stitch.

Continue as established until the black triangle in the middle is 15 sts wide. On the next front facing row work 8 sts in black as established. Work the central stitch in white stocking stitch. Tie on a new ball of black and work 8 more stitches in black.

Continue as established and make a white vee in the centre in stocking stitch while maintaining the black patterned vee.

Continue using the graph ignoring the flowers. Work the leaves from the graph or add them later with swiss darning or duplicate stitch.

Back Neck Shaping

Work the back neck as follows: put the central 21 sts on a holder and work two sts together at each neck edge each row five times till 33 sts remain. Cast off. Work other shoulder to match.

Front

Work as for back until 25 rows remain. Put the central 21 sts on a holder and work two sts together at each neck edge each front facing row five times until 33 sts remain. Continue straight until graph is complete.

Cast off.
Work other shoulder to match.

Sleeves

Cast on 42 sts for pullover or 49 sts for tunic using (A) and work cabled ribbing as for bands.

Change to body needles and increase to 50 sts. Increase one each edge every 4th row until 22 increases on each side (94 sts) or until the sleeve is desired length.

Option: when sleeve is 1" less than the desired length work one row in black stocking stitch and then work black pattern for 8 rows. For a slimmer line do not add black strip at top of sleeve. Cast off loosely.

Neckband

Using the neck band needles, (C) and the right side facing, pick up and knit 20 sts down the side of the front neck, 21 sts from the centre front, pick up 19 sts from the remaining front diagonal and then the 31 sts from the back of the neck. (91 sts).

Work the cable rib for 24 rows. Cast off loosely.

Fold the neck inside and stitch down or leave high as desired.

Leaves

Using an embroidery needle and the green mohair for the leaves work in swiss darning or duplicate stitch over the top of the knitted stitches.

Add stalks if desired as follows: with black yarn come up at the base of the leaf. Lay the thread along the path to the tip of the leaf and go back underneath. Secure it and adjust the curve by working a small loop over the laid thread by going up and back down through the same hole every 3 or 4 sts.

Finishing

Sew the side seams and arm seams neatly. Set sleeves deeply. Work in all tails. Press gently from the wrong side.

Flowers

Using Cotton Soft and a crochet hook, leave a 12" tail. Make a chain about 30 sts long. Single crochet back into the 3rd stitch, *chain 5, single crochet into the 3rd stitch* repeat from * to * until end of chain. Cut tail leaving 12". Pull through final loop.

Wind the flower into a spiral, place near a leaf and stitch in position using the tails. This is also a good opportunity to put the tails away.

Make the second flower smaller using a slightly shorter length of yarn.

Experiment with fewer chains in between each single crochet and a more open spiral for a flatter flower.

Add more flowers and buds as desired.

For a more conservative flower, chain stitch directly onto the sweater following the spiral on the graph.

Option: Add small pearls or pearl buttons to centre of flowers. You may also wish to embroider silver chainette french knots above the flowers.

New England Coat

A combination of simple oversized cables is worked with any four Encore and Galway yarns used together to make a warm, thick coat in a weekend. Make a full length or car length coat in two different colorways.

Plymouth Yarns Required
For full length coat
(100 gm balls)
(A) ENCORE #217 black x 9
(B) ENCORE #504 eggplant x 9
(C) ENCORE #473 teal mix x 9
(D) GALWAY #704 charcoal x 9
(used 4 together)

Yarns Required
For car length coat
(100 gm balls)
(A) ENCORE #9407 raspberry x 5
(B) ENCORE #9410 winesap x 5
(C) GALWAY #68 paprika x 5
(D) GALWAY #717 plum tweed x 5
(used 4 together)

Needles
U.S. #17 for long coat
10 mm (U.S. # 15, U.K.#) for
car coat
(You may prefer to work car coat
on smaller needles. This will give
a firmer jacket feel)

Stitches Used
"Mock Cable" (MC)
Skip one stitch, knit into the
second stitch leaving it on the
needle; then knit the skipped
stitch and slip both from the
needle together. Skip one stitch,
knit into the back of the second
stitch leaving it on the needle;
then knit the skipped stitch and
slip both from the needle
together. This is a four stitch,
four row repeat.

"Four Stitch Cable to the Right"
(FSCR)
Use 4 sts and cable every 8th row
as follows: Put 2 sts on a cable
needle, hold to BACK, knit 2 off
needles, knit 2 off cable needle.

"Four Stitch Cable to the Left"
(FSCL)
Use 4 sts and cable every 8th row
as follows: Put 2 sts on holder,
hold to FRONT, knit 2 off
needles, knit 2 off cable needle.

"Giant Cable"
Use 16 sts and cable every 8th
row as follows: put 2 on cable
needle, hold to BACK, K2, K 2
from cable needle. Repeat again.
Put 2 sts on cable needle, hold
to the FRONT, K2, K2 from the
cable needle. Repeat again.

"Bottom Band Cable" (BBC)
Use 8 sts and cable every 4th
row as follows: put 2 sts on cable
needle, hold to BACK, knit next
2 sts, knit 2 from cable needle,
put next 2 on cable needle, hold
to FRONT, knit next 2 sts, knit 2
from cable needle.

"Front Band Cable" (FBC)
Use 12 sts. The 8 sts from the
(BBC) continue to cross every
4th row. The other 4 sts are
either (FSCL) or (FSCR)

Back
Cast on 60 sts.
Row 1: Right side facing: K 14
(for stocking stitch at side), P2,
K4 (for mock cable) , P2, K16
(for giant cable) , P2, K4 (for
mock cable) , P2, K14 for
stocking stitch at side.

Row 2 , 4, 6 and 8: P14, K2, P4,
K2, P16, K2, P4, K2. P14

Row 3: Giant cable row: K 14,
P2, (MC), P2, giant cable , P2,
(MC), P2, K14. (60 sts).
Row 5: as row 1

Row 7: Mock cable row: K14,
P2, (MC), P2, K4, (FSCR), (FSCL),
K4, P2, (MC), P2, K14. (60 sts).

Repeat these eight rows till back
measures 15" for car coat length
or 32" for full length.

Continue body and cast on
22 sts each side to make sleeve
underarms. (104 sts) Stocking
stitch these 22 sts and maintain
cables as established for 30 rows.
Put 48 sts from arm and shoulder
on one holder. Cast off center 8
sts. Put remaining 48 sts from
other arm and shoulder on
another holder.

Left Front (while wearing)
Begin with the (BBC) which is
worked separately until it is long
enough to reach all of the way to
the centre back. At this point the
sts are cast on for the front and
the (BBC) forms a curved corner.
The (BBC) now becomes part of
the wider front band.

Cast on 8 sts for the front band
cable (FBC).
Row 1: Knit
Row 2: Purl
Row 3: work cable row
Row 4: Purl

Repeat these 4 rows for 33"

ending on row 4 of the 4 row pattern repeat.

Next row: (Front side facing) Cast on 26 more sts to the right while facing (34).

Row 1 and 5: Work 8 row pattern repeat. K14, P2, K4 , P2, K12 (34 sts). These last 12 knit sts become the larger front band cable.

Row 2, 4, 6, 8: P12 (front band cable) K2, P4 (MC), K2, P14.
Row 3: K14, P2, (MC), P2, (FSCR), (BBC).
Row 7: K14, P2, (MC), P2, K4, (BBC).

Continue as for back for a total of 3" for car coat or 23" for full length coat.

Pocket Band
Work outside 4 sts in (FSCR) for 10 rows. Return to pattern adding on sts for the sleeve as for back. Continue as established.

Neck Shaping
Continue until 30 rows from end. Begin shaping the neckband by working together the 2 rev st sts. Decrease in between the (FBC) and the (MC) by working 2 sts tog every 4th row 3 times. Continue straight until front matches back in length.

Neckband
Put all sts except the (12 sts) front band cable sts on a holder. Continue on the front band cable sts for 10 more rows ending with a stocking stitch row for ease of grafting. Leave a long tail for grafting. Place on another holder.

Right Front (while wearing)
Work as other front reversing the pattern and use the (FSLC). Buttonholes are formed naturally

in centre of every giant cable.

Top Sleeve Seam
Graft top of sleeve and shoulder sts invisibly. Leave the front band cable on the holder.

Collar
Undo rows as necessary to make (FBC) meet at back of neck. Graft together invisibly so cable pattern continues uninterrupted around the neck. Sew edge of neckband to the 8 cast off sts from centre back.

Cuff
Cast on 8 sts. Work 5 repeats of (BBC), graft into a ring. Gather edge of sleeve. Sew cable to edge.

Pocket Linings
Sew side seams leaving the pocket edging open. Cast on 20 sts and stocking stitch for 30 rows using only two thicknesses of yarn. Cast off.
Sew pocket as follows: Sew cast off edge of pocket to inside front in line with the top of the pocket edging. Sew side of pocket to

side seam of back. Sew remaining two sides to inside front with the bottom of the pocket 10 rows below the pocket edging. Sew on buttons if desired.

Hat
Use your leftovers to make a pretty pull-on hat that cables its way around your head.

Work sideways. Cast on 30 sts.
Row 1: K16, P2 purl, K 12 sts.
Row 2 and 4: P12, K2, P16.
Row 3: K8, (BBC), P2, K8, turn leaving the last 4 sts on needle. This makes a short row to shape crown.

Continue for 60 rows or what ever length is required to go around head.

Cast off. Sew cast on row to cast off row invisibly or do not cast off and graft to cast on row instead. Fold stocking stitch 8 sts under and stitch to 2 sts of reverse stocking stitch. Gather the short row edge into a tight circle at crown using darning needle. Sew firmly.

Car Coat

Fabiola Lily

Beautiful varieties of irises and lilies grow in lily ponds and attract delicate dragonflies and butterflies in summer. This cotton tunic with the vertical lines and colour up by the face is designed to be especially flattering on fuller figures. The lace edging adds a touch of Victorian romance to the playfully sensuous scooped neck. The knitted lace also drapes over the hands or flips back for a more practical effect. It may be knitted on a black or white background. The pattern for a standard sweater is also provided.

Plymouth Yarns Required for Black Fabiola Lily Tunic
All COTTON SOFT (50 gm balls)
- (A) #899 black x 16
- (B) #573 light green x 1
- (C) #9003 green x 1
- (D) #062 dark green x 1
- (E) #800 white x 1
- (F) #843 grey x 1
- (G) gold metallic x 1
- (H) #319 hot pink x 16 yds
- (I) same as (H)
- (J) #361 red x 14 yds
- (K) #339 orange x 5 yds
- (L) #709 yellow x 5 yds
- (M) #628 purple x 1
- (N) #631 lilac x 5 yds
- (P) green metallic x 5 yds
- (Q) silver chainette x 8 yds
- (R) #616 red berry x 10 yds
- (S) black metallic x 10 yds
- (T) purple metallic x 12 yds

Plymouth Yarns Required for White Fabiola Lily Tunic
All "Cotton Soft" and "Colorburst" in 50 gm balls
- (A) #800 white x 16
- (B) #899 black x 1
- (C) #9003 Colorburst green x 1
- (D) #062 dark green x 1
- (E) same as C
- (F) #843 grey x 1
- (G) gold chainette x 1
- (I) #319 hot pink x 16 yds
- (J) #361 red x 14 yds
- (K) #339 orange x 5 yds
- (L) #709 yellow x 5 yds
- (M) #628 purple x 1
- (N) #631 lilac x 5 yds
- (P) green metallic x 5 yds
- (Q) silver chainette x 8 yds
- (R) #616 red berry x 10 yds
- (S) black metallic x 10 yds
- (T) purple metallic x 12 yds

Needles

4¹/₂ mm (U.S. #7, U.K. #7 for body or as required to achieve gauge

Tension or Gauge

20 sts to 4" or 10 cm
27 rows to 4" or 10 cm

Garment Size

Length = 26" or 66 cm plus knitted lace
Width = 24" or 61 cm

Back

Cast on loosely 120 sts in black or white using body needles. Work 180 rows of graph in stocking stitch.

Front

Cast on as for back. Work graph for 160 rows. Shape neck as shown on graph. Cast off.

Sleeves

Cast on 56 sts and use the sleeve graph. Increase one each side every 6th row. When graph is completed, continue increasing until sleeve is desired length. Remember, the wider the tunic the shorter the sleeves. Cast off loosely.

Lace Edging

Knit a "WILLOW" lace edge for bottom and for sleeve.

Knit the lace sideways. Cast on 10 sts using black (or white) and 4 mm needles.

Row 1: Slip 1, K2, YO (Yarn forward and over needle), K2 tog, (YO twice K2 tog) twice, K1 =10 stitches.

Row 2: K2, (K1,P1 into the two loops of the double YO, K1) twice, K1, YO, K2 tog, K1 = 12 stitches.

Row 3: Slip1, K2, YO, K2tog, K2, (YO twice, K2 tog) twice, K1.

Row 4: K2, (K1,P1 into the two loops of the double YO, K1) twice, K3,YO, K2 tog, K1, =14 stitches.

Row 5: Slip1, K2, YO, K2 tog, K4, (YO twice, K2 tog,) twice, K1.

Row 6: K2, (K1, P1 into the two loops of the double YO, K1) twice, K5, YO, K2 tog, K1, = 16 stitches.

Row 7: slip 1, K2, YO, K2 tog, K11.

Row 8: cast off 6 sts, K6 not including the st already on the needle after the cast off, YO, K2 tog, K1.

Repeat these eight rows for as long as necessary to match cast on row of body without gathering. Sew on to body with black or white open faggot stitch.

Lace at Neckline

Knit the lace sideways.

Cast on 6 sts using black or required colour and 4 mm needles.

Row 1: (right side): Slip 1, K2,YO (yarn forward and over needle = YO), K2 tog, slip 1.

Row 2: Knit into 1st stitch and place this new stitch back onto the left needle. Repeat this 3 more times making 4 sts or a total of 10 sts on the left hand needle. Knit these 4 sts onto the right hand needle and drop the 5th stitch which is the stitch you began with.

With the left needle lift the 2nd stitch on the right needle over the 1st stitch and off the needle. Repeat taking the 3rd stitch over and off the same stitch and then the 4th stitch over and off, leaving 1 stitch on the right hand needle to replace the dropped stitch. This completes the picot knot. K2, YO, K2 together, K1.

Row 3: repeat row 1
Row 4: K3, YO, K2 tog, K1.

Repeat these 4 rows for as long as needed to go around the scooped neck.

With the picot knot facing down and over the front edge of the sweater neck and the straight edge of the edging above the sweater neckline, back stitch this edging onto the neckline with black metallic.

Finishing
Sew sleeves and side seams. Check all tails are sewn in firmly. Press gently.

Standard Pullover
(20" or 51 cm wide and 24" or 61 cm long)

Cast on 90 sts, rib 3". Increase to 100 sts. Leave 10 sts off each side of the graph and leave 40 rows off bottom of graph. Five rows from end put central 20 sts on holder. Work 2 tog at neck edges each row 5 times. Cast off shoulders.

Front neckline: 25 rows from the end put centre 20 sts on holder, work 2 tog at neck edge 5 times then cont straight till front matches back in length.

Sleeves
Cast on 40 sts, rib 3" increase to 56 sts. Work graph.

Neckband
Pick up 70 sts around neck and rib 20 rows. Cast off and fold outside. Stitch down.

Sew sleeves and side seams. Set sleeves deeply.

Sew in tails and press gently.

Intersecting Diamonds

Eleven different rays of Plymouth Galway and Cotton Soft colours intersect in the centre and form bright diamonds. The deep vee is set on a black background on a tunic shape to create a fun, flattering and comfortable garment.

Plymouth Yarns Required

COTTON SOFT = 50 gm balls
GALWAY = 100 gm hanks

(A) COTTON SOFT #339 peach x 1
(B) COTTON SOFT #612 cool pink x 1
(C) COTTON SOFT #624 ash rose x 1
(D) COTTON SOFT #628 purple x 1
(E) COTTON SOFT #034 blue x 1
(F) GALWAY #11 cobalt blue x 1
(G) GALWAY #707 heather green x 1
(H) GALWAY #705 heather navy x 1
(I) GALWAY #704 charcoal x 1
(J) GALWAY #18 dark teal x 1
(K) GALWAY #15 blue grey x 1
(L) GALWAY #9 black x 4 (6)

Needles

Cuffs and neckband: 4 mm
(U.S. #6, U.K. #7 or 8)
Bottom inside band on body:
4 $\frac{1}{2}$ mm (U.S. #7, U.K. #6 or #7)
Body: 5 mm (U.S. #8, U.K #6)

Tension or Gauge

18 sts and 24 rows to 4" or 10 cm

Garment Size

Small/Medium (photographed)
Width: 95 sts = 21$\frac{1}{2}$" or 55 cm
Length: approx 160 rows = 26$\frac{1}{2}$" or 68 cm

Medium/Large
Width: 115 sts = 25$\frac{3}{4}$" or 65 cm
Length: approx 160 rows = 26$\frac{1}{2}$" or 68 cm

Add 10 sts each side for a larger hip measurement.

Back

Using inside bottom band needles and (L) cast on 95 (115) sts.
Stocking stitch (knit the front

facing rows and purl the back facing rows =st st) for 10 rows. Do one row in reverse st st as a turning row. Change to body needles. Work the additional 20 stitches for larger size as 10 black stitches on each side of graph. St st 36 rows for the shorter length as photographed. Work an additional 20 rows before beginning the first diamond if you would like a longer tunic, or are taller than 5' 3". Make sure the first row of the graph is a front facing knit row so all purl rows are simply a repeat of the row below.

If you have begun with the larger hip measurement, decrease up the sides as follows: Work 2 tog each outside edge every 10th row till 95 stitches then continue straight as for smaller size till armholes.

Armhole

Cast off the first and last 8 sts.

Begin the decrease for the

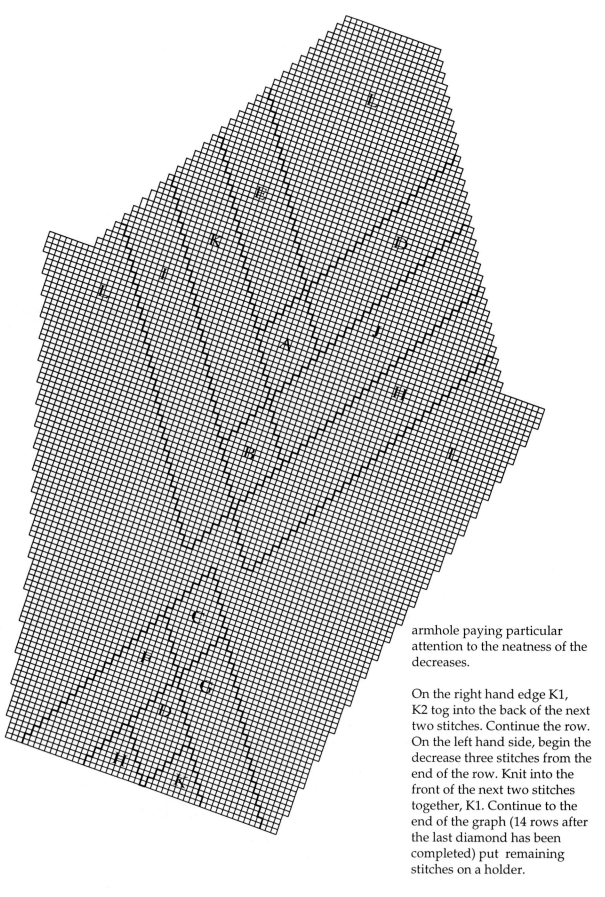

armhole paying particular attention to the neatness of the decreases.

On the right hand edge K1, K2 tog into the back of the next two stitches. Continue the row. On the left hand side, begin the decrease three stitches from the end of the row. Knit into the front of the next two stitches together, K1. Continue to the end of the graph (14 rows after the last diamond has been completed) put remaining stitches on a holder.

Front

Work as for back until two rows after the last diamond. Put the central 11 sts on a holder. K2 tog at neck edge each front facing row five times (0 sts rem).

Sleeves

Using band needles, cast on 36 sts for a small wrist, (as photographed) 42 for a medium wrist and 47 sts for a large wrist, in (L). Work as for bottom band. Next wrong side facing row change to body needles. Increase evenly to 49 sts. Begin graph. Increase one each edge on the 4th row, then every 6th row 5 times. Inc every 4th row until reaching the armholes (91 sts). Add length at the gap in the middle if necessary but do not increase to more than 91 sts.

Arm Hole

Cast off the first and last 8 sts. Begin the decreases for the armhole. Continue working the graph until 17 sts remain. Put them on a holder.

Neckband

Sew shoulder seams. Using the neck band needles, (L) and the right side facing, pick up and knit the 17 sts from one arm, 12 sts down the diagonal of the front neck, 11 sts from the centre front, and 12 sts from the remaining front diagonal. Knit up the stitches from the remaining sleeve and then the 21 sts from the back of the neck. (90 sts)
Rib for 12 rows in (L) then 10 rows in (B). Cast off loosely.

Finishing

Press gently from the wrong side. Sew the side seams and underarm seams neatly. Sew the diagonal armhole seams. Change colour each time and match either of the two colours being joined. Fold in the cotton bands and stitch along the inside edge.

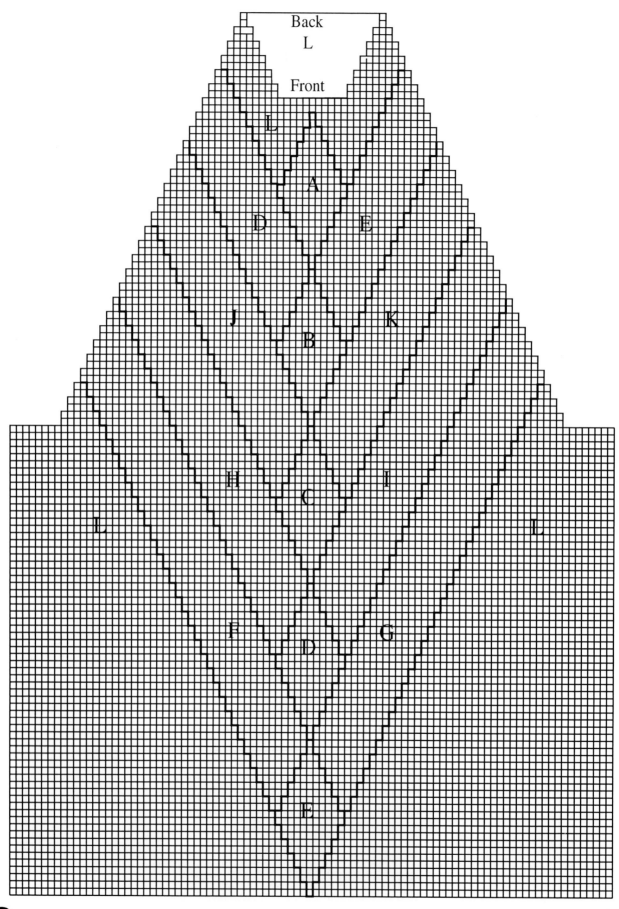

Galway and Cotton Soft

Statue

Classic neutral colours in a dramatic design make this garment a rewarding project for any knitter. It is worked in machine washable Plymouth Encore used double throughout on large needles. Simple black chain stitch worked separately outlines the colour changes making it even more 'forgiving'. Use extra large needles for a casual 'oversized cardigan', or smaller needles for a firmer, more formal 'jacket'.

Plymouth Yarns Required

(100 gm balls) enough for both sizes
(A), (B) and (C) yarns ARE USED DOUBLED THROUGH OUT
(D) IS USED TRIPLE THROUGHOUT
(A) ENCORE #194 grey heather x 4
(B) ENCORE #208 white x 5
(C) ENCORE #240 taupe x 3
(D) ENCORE #217 black x 2

Small/Medium Size
Needles
4 mm (U.S. #6, U.K. #8) for the bands
5.5 mm (U.S. #10, U.K. #4) for the body

Tension or Gauge
15.5 sts to 4" or 10 cm
18 rows to 4" or 10 cm

Garment Size
Width: 90 sts = 23" or 59 cm
Length: 2^1/$_2$" or 79 cm

Medium/Large Size
Needles
5 mm (U.S. #9, U.K. #5) for the bands
6.5 mm (U.S. #10^1/$_2$, U.K. #3) for the body

Tension or Gauge
14 sts to 4" or 10 cm
17 rows to 4" or 10 cm

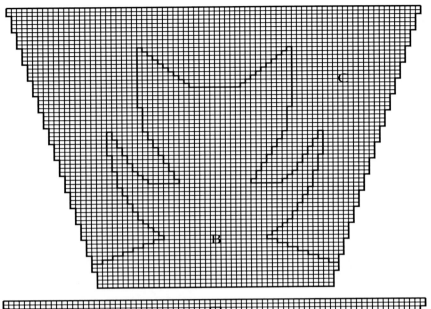

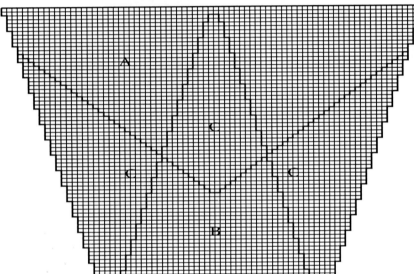

Pocket Edging

After 30 graph rows work the outside 4 sts in garter st (knit every row) for 20 rows to form the pocket edging. Continue straight till 25 rows from the end.

Neckhole

Work two together at the neck edge each front facing row until 34 sts remain. Continue straight until front matches the back. Cast off.

Work other front to match using the second graph.

Sleeves

Using band needles and grey (A) DOUBLED cast on 30 sts. Work as bottom band, then work black "knitted in edging" again but increase evenly 10 sts to 46 sts on the final wrong side facing row.

Change to body needles. Begin the graph. Increase one each edge every 4th row while working the graph or to desired length. Cast off loosely. Work other sleeve using second sleeve graph.

Collar

Sew shoulder seams. With front side facing and using black knit up 5 sts from the cast off sts, 11 sts along the diagonal, 14 sts along back of neck, 16 down the remaining front = 46 sts. Knit row 1 on wrong side facing row. Purl row 2. Knit row 3. Change to grey. Knit 1st row and continue for 9 more rows in st st.

On front side facing row knit one row in black. At end of row cast on an extra 5 sts in black to make top of front band.
Row 2: Knit wrong side facing row and add on 5 more black sts.
Row 3: Purl right side row.
Row 4: Knit wrong side facing row. Change to grey and knit

Garment Size

Width: 90 sts = 26" or 64 cm
Length: = 31^1/$_4$"

Back

Using band needles and grey (A) DOUBLED cast on 80 sts. Stocking stitch for 10 rows to make inside part of folded band.

Work one row in purl on a front facing row for fold. Continue in stocking stitch for 12 rows.

On next front facing row using black tripled, work the "knitted in edging" as follows:
K row 1, K row 2, P row 3.

On the next wrong side facing row, using black, evenly increase 10 sts to 90 sts.

Change to body needles. Begin the graph. Continue straight until back neck shaping (5 rows from end). Put the central 12 sts on a holder. Work 2 tog at the neck edge on every row 5 times until 34 sts remain. Cast off shoulder. Work other shoulder to match.

Front

Cast on 36 sts in grey. Work as bottom band. Increase to 40 sts. Begin first front graph.

right side facing row leaving the 5 black sts at each end on holder. Continue for 9 more rows in st st. Cast off in grey. Fold in half and stitch in place.

Front Button Band

With front side facing using grey knit up 4 sts from the collar, 5 sts for every 7 rows along the front and one stitch every 2nd row along the bottom band. Work 9 rows in grey. Work one row in purl on right side facing row to make fold. Work 8 rows in grey stocking stitch. Cast off in grey. Fold in half and stitch in place.

Front Buttonhole Band

Work as other front band till row 5. Work a buttonhole row as follows: Knit 4 sts, *yarn over, K2 tog, K13*. Repeat from * to * six more times. Complete the 4 rows in grey.

Continue as for other front. Work second button hole row to line up with first. Complete band. Fold in half and stitch in place.

Embroidery

Outline all colour changes along band to body in black chain stitch using three strands of black crochet with a large hook. Sew on 7 black buttons.

Pocket Linings

Sew side seams leaving the pocket edging open. Cast on 20 sts (use single) in (C) for one pocket and (A) for the other. St st for 30 rows. Cast off. Sew top to inside front in line with the top of the pocket edging.

Sew side of pocket to side seam of back. Sew remaining two sides to inside front with the bottom of the pocket 10 rows below the pocket edging.

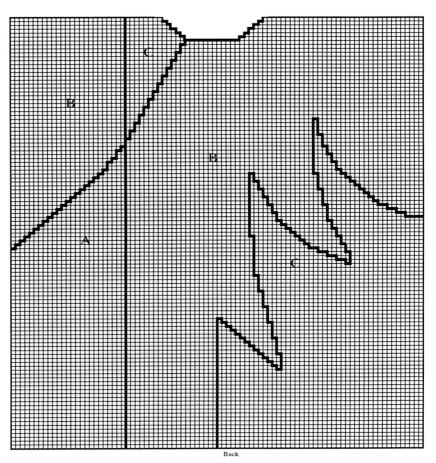

Back

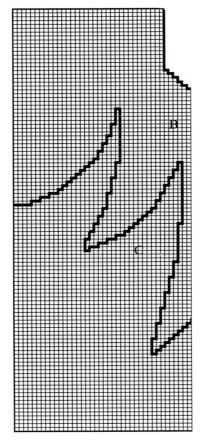

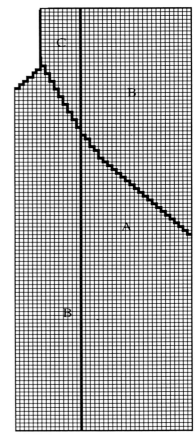

Cropped Vineyard

Diamonds divided into three leaf colours and outlined in a paprika lattice combine into a bold geometric pattern in a young cropped pullover. Instructions also include a fuller, longer tunic pattern.

Plymouth Yarns Required
(100 gm hanks)
(yarns and instructions for tunic in brackets)
(A) GALWAY #714 heather green x 1 (3)
(B) GALWAY #65 dark green x 2 (4)
(C) GALWAY #59 olive x 2 (4)
(D) GALWAY #68 paprika x 2 (5)

Needles
$4^{1}/_{2}$ mm (U.S. #8, U.K. #6)
Size 6 crochet hook

Tension or Gauge for both pullover and tunic
20 sts to 4" or 10 cm
28 rows to 4" or 10 cm

Garment Size
Width at armhole
Pullover: 91 sts = 18" or 46 cm
Tunic: 121 sts = 24" or 61 cm
Length: cropped Pullover: 95 graph rows plus 1" ban = $14^{1}/_{2}$" or 37 cm
Standard Pullover: 150 graph rows plus 1' band = $22^{1}/_{2}$" or 56 cm
Tunic: 180 graph rows plus 1" band = 27" or 69 cm

Back
Cast on 71 (121) sts using paprika and work one knit row and one purl row.
Row 1 of graph: Take care when joining on colours for the first row the of graph as this establishes the pattern. Use 2 to 3 yd lengths and pull the tails through the tangle as you work. Work in stocking stitch (knit front facing

row and purl back facing rows) The graph is 30 sts wide and 60 rows long. The pullover is shown as a cropped style however each new diamond adds about 9 inches or 22 cm to the length.

First graph row for cropped pullover
Tie on (C). Work the final 5 sts of the graph, the full graph twice and then the first 6 sts of the graph once = (71 sts). Increase one each edge every 6th row (89 sts). Continue straight until graph has been worked one and a half times (approx 95 rows) for the cropped pullover as shown, or as desired. The pattern on the shoulders will line up regardless of the length. For a standard length pullover work two and a half full diamonds.

First graph row for tunic
Tie on (B). Work the full graph 4 times. Continue straight until three full diamonds have been completed (or as desired). Cast off.

Front
Work as for back until 40 rows remain. Put the central stitch on a holder. Complete row. Work two sts together at each neck edge every front facing row until length matches back.

Sleeves
Cast on 41 (51) sts. For slim sleeve style on pullover begin with final 5 sts of graph, work one graph and then work the first 6 sts. For a slightly fuller sleeve for the tunic or pullover work the last 10 sts of the graph, the full graph and then the first 11 sts. Increase one each edge every 6th row for two full diamond repeats (or as desired) for the pullover. Increase at the same rate but for only one and half diamonds (or as desired) for

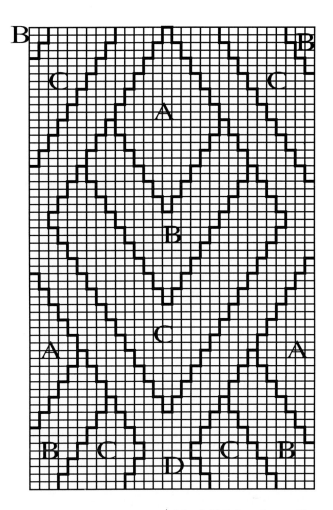

the tunic, as it is wider. Cast off loosely. The sleeve design does not line up with any particular part of the body so don't worry about this.

Bottom and Cuff Edging for pullover and tunic
Work crochet edges using size 6 crochet hook and a basic single crochet stitch and paprika.

Cuff
Work into every stitch on cuff for a total of 2 rows or until edge appears to match the width of the paprika diagonals in body.

Body
Work into every stitch on body for first row then skip every 6th stitch on next row. Work one or two more rows.

Sew shoulder seams.

Neck Edging for pullover and tunic
Crochet into every stitch along the back of neck, once into every row on front diagonal and every stitch on holder, then into every row on final diagonal.
Second Crochet Row
Work into every 2nd stitch across back of neck, every stitch on diagonal, skip the three central stitches at bottom of vee and then into every stitch on final diagonal.
Third Crochet Row
Work into every stitch but skip one stitch at central vee.
Final Crochet Row
As previous row.
Make separate small chain and sew vertically along centre vee to complete neckband.

Finishing
Set sleeves in deeply. Sew remaining tails. Press.

Deca

Deca uses the interplay of ten colours. It is easy and satisfying to knit. Vertical lines are the easiest type of intarsia work because they untangle themselves as they go, and once the new set of colours are tied on, the following rows for the blocks are all the same. The square inset shoulder is defined by a simple line.

The basic Deca pattern may also be adapted in a textured garment using different types of decorative stitch patterns for each of the squares, like a sampler. As different stitch types cause different distortions the blocks will no longer be square. Choose the different stitch types so they balance out in the end and press the garment carefully before sewing the side seams.

Plymouth Yarns Required
(100 gm hanks)
Red Deca
(A) GALWAY #10 navy x 1
(B) GALWAY #704 charcoal x 1
(C) GALWAY #13 grape x 1
(D) GALWAY #44 red x 1
(E) GALWAY #710 heather red x 1
(F) GALWAY #703 heather green x 1
(G) GALWAY #707 heather mint x 1
(H) GALWAY #09 black x 1
(I) GALWAY #706 heather blue x 1
(J) GALWAY #705 heather navy x 1

Yarns Required
Denim Deca
(A) GALWAY #709 denim blue x 1
(B) GALWAY #15 lilac x 1
(C) GALWAY #14 lilac grey x 1
(D) GALWAY #715 light heather
      turquoise x 1
(E) GALWAY #18 dark teal x 1
(F) GALWAY #704 charcoal x 1
(G) GALWAY #22 cerulean blue x 1
(H) GALWAY #707 heather mint x 1
(I) GALWAY #11 cobalt x 1
(J) GALWAY #706 heather blue x 1

Needles
3¹/₂ mm (U.S. #4, U.K. #9 or #10)
for the bands and a circular
needle of the same size for the
neck bands
4¹/₂ mm (U.S. #7, U.K. #7) for
the body

Tension or Gauge
20 sts and 27 rows to 4" or 10 cm

Red Deca colourway shown above.

Blue Denim colourway shown above.

diagram. Keep the yarn 'cross overs' at the colour changes firm. Add an extra row of blocks to the body and the sleeves for an extra tall person.

Armhole

Cast off the first block using the matching yarn for all but the last stitch. Use the colour of the next block for this final stitch. Cut the yarn for the cast off block leaving a sewing up tail. Continue the row and use the matching yarn to cast off the last block. Cut yarn leaving a tail for sewing up. Continue the diagram for the next three layers of blocks. At 5 rows from the end of the final block work the back neck shaping as follows:

Put the centre 20 sts of a holder. Work 2 together at the neck edges every row five times. Cast off using matching colours for all but the last stitch of each block. Use the colour of the next block for this final stitch. Cut the yarn for each block leaving a tail for sewing up.

Front

As back until 5 rows from the end of the second to last layer of blocks. Put all the stitches from the centre block on a holder. Work two together at the neck edge each front facing row five times. Continue straight until the final layer of blocks is completed.

Sleeves

Cast on 54, (56, 58) sts and work ribbing as for bands. Change to body needles and stocking stitch and increase to 64 (68, 72) sts. Begin first layers of blocks. Increase one each edge on the 4th row and then every 6th row thereafter until 4 layers of blocks have been completed. Work the 5th layer without increasing.

Garment Size

Body: 7 blocks wide and 8 blocks long plus band
Sleeve: 5 blocks long plus cuff and top stripe.

SMALL
Each block: 16 sts and 20 rows
Width: 112 sts = 22" or 56 cm
Length: 181 rows (160 plus 21 rows in band) = 26 $1/2$" or 67 cm

MEDIUM
Block: 17 sts and 21 rows
Width: 119 sts = 23 $3/4$" or 60 cm
Length: 189 rows (168 plus 21 rows in band) = 28"or 71 cm

LARGE
Block: 18 sts and 22 rows
Width: 126 sts = 25$1/2$" or 65 cm
Length: 197 rows (176 plus 21 rows in band) = 29" or 74 cm

Back

Using band needles and (H) cast on 104 (110, 118) sts. Rib (K1, P1 across row every row) for 7 rows. Change to (A) and continue ribbing for 7 rows. Change to (J) and rib 7 more rows. On the next purl row increase 8 or 9 sts as required to 112 (119, 126) sts and change to body needles and stocking stitch knit the front facing rows and purl the back facing rows).

Work each block as follows:
Small men's: 16 sts and 20 rows
Medium men's: 17 sts and 21 rows.
Large men's: 18 sts and 22 rows.

Take care when tying on yarns for first body row.
Use the colours specified on the

Work 7 rows in black. Cast off loosely.

Neckband

Using circular needles pick up and knit 79 sts around neck hole, rib 7 rows in (J), 7 in (and A), 7 in (H). Cast off, fold in and stitch down.

Additional Colourway (not shown)

Deca Light

This is a light, natural group of colours. The denim blue, olive and heather plum have been added to make the sweater work with jeans and khaki pants. Men tend to ask for a burgundy or plum colour too.

(A)   GALWAY #717 heather plum x 1
(B)   GALWAY # 58 olive x 1
(C)   GALWAY # 702 light grey x 1
(D)   GALWAY # 03 warm beige x 1
(E)   GALWAY # 01 cream x 1
(F)   GALWAY # 704 charcoal x 1
(G)   GALWAY # 711 natural brown x 1
(H)   GALWAY # 09 black x 1
(I)   GALWAY # 27 soft grey green x 1
(J)   GALWAY # 709 denim blue x 1

Blue Denim colourway shown above.

Wanyama Wakubwa

"Wanyama Wakubwa" means big animals in Swahili. The black abstract animals on a copper background is typical of the simple printed images on cotton fabrics from Kenya.

Plymouth Yarns Required
(100 gm balls)
(A) ENCORE #223 brown x 7 (8, 8)
(B) ENCORE #217 black x 2

Needles
3¹/₂ mm (U.S. #4, U.K. #9 or #10) for the bands
Circular needle of the same size for the neck bands
4 or 4¹/₂ mm (U.S. #7 or #6, U.K. #7 or #8) for the body

Tension or Gauge
20 sts to 4" or 10 cm
27 rows to 4" or 10 cm

Garment Size
Width: 100 (110, 120) sts = 20" or 50 cm (22" or 55 cm, 24" or 61 cm)
Length: 150 (160) rows of graph = (25" or 64 cm, 27" or 69 cm)

Front
Using band needles and (A) (copper brown) cast on 90 (100, 110) sts. Rib (K1, P1 across row every row) for 21 rows or 3". On the next purl row increase 10 sts to 100 (110, 120) sts and change to body needles and stocking stitch (Knit the front facing rows and purl the back facing rows.)

On a front facing row begin the graph. Ignore the first 10 rows of graph for the shorter length. Ignore the outside 10 (5, 0) sts on each side, to make the width required.

Continue until 25 rows from the end. Put the 18 central stitches on a holder. Work two together at the neck edges each front facing row five times. Continue straight for 15 rows. Cast off. Work other shoulder to match.

Back
Work as for front until graph. Work back in background yarn randomly positioning approximately 10 black squares (each 5 sts and 6 rows — like the two on the front.) Continue until 5 rows from the end. Begin back neck shaping. Put the central 18 sts on a holder. Work 2 tog at the neck edge on each row 5 times. Cast off. Work other shoulder to match.

Sleeve
Cast on 48 sts using (A) and work ribbing as for bands. Change to body needles and stocking stitch and increase to 53 sts. Increase one each edge every 4th row while working the graph of the palm trees and squares. If graph finishes before desired length continue on background colour. Cast off loosely.

Neckband
Sew shoulders. Using circular needles pick up and knit 92 sts around neck hole. Rib 21 rows as bottom band. Cast off, fold in and stitch down.

Set sleeves in deeply. Sew sleeve and side seams. Put all tails away. Press gently.

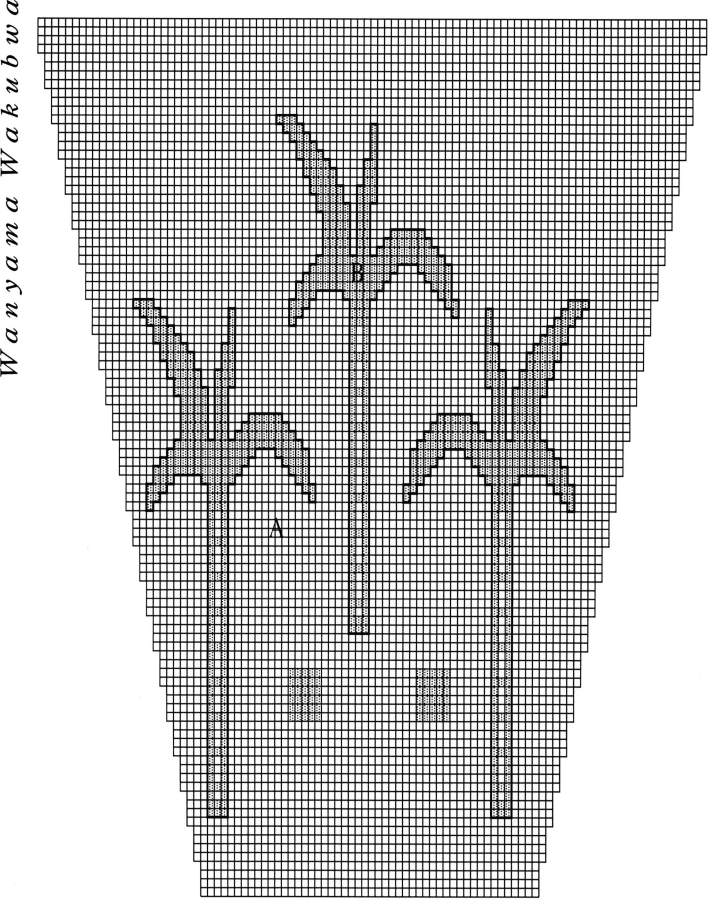

Photo shows bright colourway in Cotton Soft.

Galway and Cotton Soft

Energy

Eleven bright colours combine in an energetic pattern of spirals and zig zags. This graph is not for a beginner but it is rewarding for a knitter with some intarsia experience. Remember any graph is only a guide and it is the beautiful colours that will attract the attention. Have fun!

Plymouth Yarns Required
for bright wool version
(A) COTTON SOFT #339 apricot x 2
(B) GALWAY #09 black x 3
(C) GALWAY #22 cerulean blue x 1
(E) GALWAY #23 cerise x 1
(G) GALWAY #17 green x 1
(K) GALWAY #11 cobalt x 1
(N) GALWAY #10 navy x 1
(M) COTTON SOFT #612 magenta x 1
(P) GALWAY #24 purple x 2
(R) GALWAY #16 red x 1
(T) GALWAY #18 teal x 1

Plymouth Yarns Required
for bright cotton version
(A) COTTON SOFT #709 gold x 3
(B) COTTON SOFT #899 black x 1
(C) COTTON SOFT #800 white x 1
(E) COTTON SOFT #034
    cerulean blue x 1
(G) COTTON SOFT #536 green x 1
(K), (N) COTTON SOFT #358 red x 1
(M) COTTON SOFT #319
    hot pink x 1
(P) COTTON SOFT #628 purple x 2
(R) COTTON SOFT #339 apricot x 1
(T) COTTON SOFT #255 royal x 1

Plymouth Yarns Required
for bronze cotton version on man
(A) COTTON SOFT #709 gold x 3
(B) COTTONSOFT #899 black x 1
(C) COTTON SOFT #809 cream x 1
(E) COTTON SOFT #393 deep red x 1
(G) COTTON SOFT #560
    olive green x 1
(K) (N) COTTON SOFT #263 navy x 1
(M) COTTON SOFT #616
    magenta x 1
(P) COTTON SOFT #628 purple x 2
(R) COTTON SOFT #361 red x 1
(T) COTTON SOFT #843 grey x 1

Photo shows bright colourway in Galway.

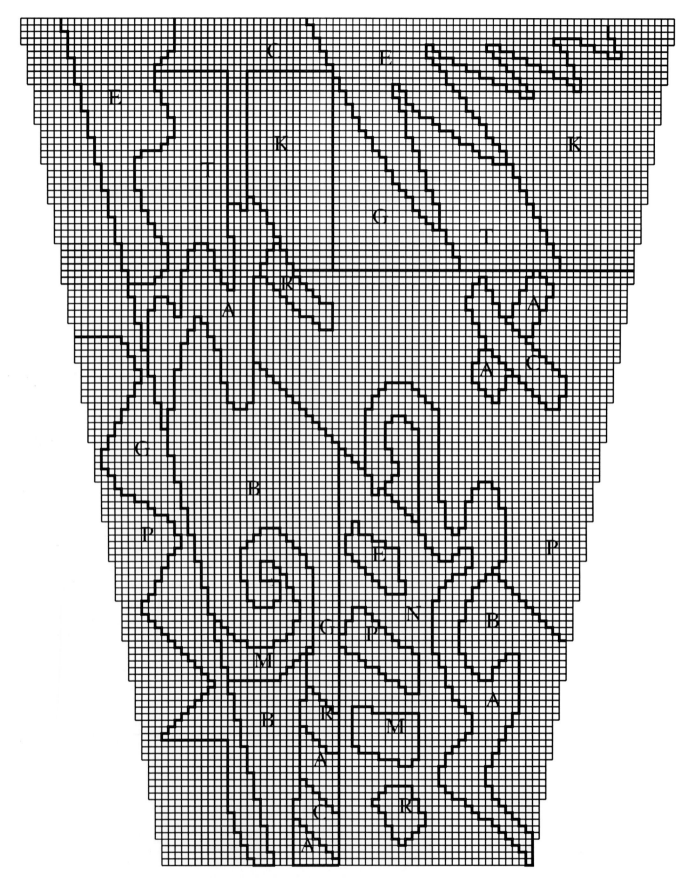

Needles

3¹/₂ mm (U.S. #4, U.K. #9 or #10)
for the bands
Circular needle as above for the
neck bands
4¹/₂ or 5 mm (U.S. #7 or #8,
U.K. #6 or #7)
for the body or as required to
achieve desired tension

Tension or Gauge

20 sts to 4" or 10 cm
27 rows to 4" or 10 cm

Garment Size

Small Width: 100 sts = 20"
or 51 cm
Medium Width: 110 sts = 22"
or 56 cm
Large Width: 120 sts = 24"
or 61 cm

Shorter Length: 153 rows of graph
plus 3" band = 25¹/₂"
or 65 cm

Medium Length: 163 rows of
graph plus 3" of band = 27"
or 69 cm

Longer Length: 173 rows of graph
plus 3" of band = 28¹/₂" or 72 cm

Back

Using band needles and (B) cast
on 90 (100, 110) sts. Rib (K1, P1
across row every row) for 21
rows. On the next purl row
increase 10 sts to 100 (110, 120)
sts. Change to body needles and
stocking stitch (knit the front
facing rows and purl the back
facing rows.) Leave outside 10
(5, 0) sts off each side of graph.
Begin 20 (10, 0) rows from bottom
of graph.

Back Neck Shaping

Five rows from end put the
central 20 sts on a holder. Work
2 tog at the neck edge on each
row 5 times. Cast off remaining 35
(40, 45) sts. Work other shoulder
to match.

Photo shows bronze colourway in Cotton Soft.

Front

As back until 25 rows from the end. Put the 16 central stitches on a holder. Work two together at the neck edge each front facing row 7 times. Continue straight until front matches the back. Cast off. Work other shoulder to match.

Sleeve

Cast on 48 sts using (B) and work ribbing as for bands. Change to body needles and st st increase to 56 sts. Increase one each edge every 6th row until sleeve is desired length. Cast off loosely.

Neckband

Sew shoulder seams.
Using circular needles pick up and knit 90 sts around neck hole and rib 21 rows in (B). Cast off all in knit or purl, fold outside and stitch down.

Finishing

Sew sleeve seam and side seams. Set sleeve deeply. Sew tails and press gently.

Photo shows bright colourway in Cotton Soft.

Photo shows bright colourway inGalway.

Clear Concept

Purple and black are a great combination but this pattern can be worked in any two colours. Make each block a different colour if you are adventurous. It can be made any length, including a shorter cropped version.

Plymouth Yarns Required
(100 gm hanks)
(A) GALWAY #09 black x 5 (6, 6)
(B) GALWAY #24 purple x 4 (5, 5)

Needles
3¹/₂ mm (U.S. #4, U.K. #9 or #10) for the bands
Circular needle of the same size for the neck bands
4 or 4¹/₂ mm (U.S. #7 or #6, U.K. #7 or #8) for the body

Tension or Gauge
20 sts to to 4" or 10 cm
27 rows to 4" or 10 cm

Garment Size
This garment is offered in one width and three lengths. The instructions for the medium and longer lengths are given in brackets.

Width: 110 sts = 56 cm or 22"
Cropped Length: 102 rows (plus 3" band) = 18" or 46 cm

Medium Length: 142 rows (plus 3" band) = 24" or 61 cm
Full Length: 182 rows (plus 3" band) = 29" or 73 cm

Back

Using band needles and (A) cast on 100 sts. Rib (K1, P1) for 21 rows. On the next purl row increase 10 sts to 110 sts. Change to body needles and stocking stitch (knit the front facing rows and purl the back facing rows.)

Row 1: (front facing row) K40 purple, tie on black, K 70 black.

Row 2: (back facing row) P70 black, P40 purple.
Continue as established until 10 (50, 90) stocking stitch rows have been worked.

Row 11 (51, 91): K20 purple, K20 black, K20 purple, K50 black.
Continue as established until 30 rows have been completed.

Row 41(81, 121): K20 black, K 20 purple, K20 black, K 50 purple.

Continue as established until 30 rows have been completed.
Row 71(111,151): K 40 black, K 70 purple. Continue as established for 23 rows.

Back Neck Shaping

Put the central 20 sts on a holder. Work 2 tog at the neck edges on each row 5 times. Work 2 rows straight. Cast off remaining 40 sts for shoulder. Work other shoulder to match.

Front

The front is not a reverse of the back. The colours will change at the side seams and shoulders but this is consistent with the 'block' nature of the design. Work as back until 25 rows from the end. Put the 20 central stitches on a holder. K2 tog at the neck edges each front facing row five times. Continue straight until front matches the back. Cast off shoulders.

Sleeve

Cast on 48 sts using black. Work ribbing as for bands. Change to body needles and stocking stitch and increase to 56 sts. Increase one each edge every 4th row until sleeve is long enough. Cast off loosely. Set deeply. Make other sleeve in purple. Attach purple sleeve to black side of front.

Neckband

Sew shoulder seams. Using a circular needle, pick up and knit 90 sts around neck hole. Rib 21 rows in (B). Cast off, fold in and stitch down.

Finishing

Sew side seams. Sew in tails. Press gently

Landscape Vest

Painters often enjoy the challenge of working with natural light as it changes a landscape from hour to hour. In this Landscape Vest random dyed yarns lend their own changes to the clouds in the sky, the shadows on the mountains, the rustling grasses and the briefly blooming and fading flowers. The vest is knitted side to side with the black frame all worked in at the same time. The lupine flowers are embroidered on later with a simple stitch in a colour changing yarn.

Plymouth Yarns Required

All COTTON SOFT
(50 gm balls)

(A) #899 black x 3 (4)
(B) #9003 grasses x 2
(C) #638 purple x 1
(D) #057 trees dark green x 1
(E) #9001 mountain lilacs x 1
(F) #9377 pastels sky x 1
(G) #034 blue x 1
(H) #9005 roses x 1

Needles

3.5 mm (U.S. #4, U.K #10) bands and body worked as one

Tension or Gauge (after pressing)

20 sts to 4" or 10 cm
27 rows to 4" or 10 cm

Garment Size

19" or 48 cm wide
23" or 58 cm long

Body

Begin with the front band. Cast on 78 sts using black. Work 10 rows in garter stitch (knit every row). Work all green stalks and black stalks that are two rows or more wide in garter stitch.

On last row increase into every 6th stitch Do not increase into the first or last 6 sts stitches (90 sts.) Keep 1st 6 sts and last 6 sts in black garter stitch.
Use graph for central 78 sts.

Work 10 rows of graph. Increase at neck edge in (F) in between the black sts and graph sts each front facing row twice.

Front Neck Shaping
On the 14th row of graph cast on 17 sts in black to make 23 sts altogether. Continue increasing at edge between black and graph until 6 sts have been increased and 9 rows of black garter stitch have been worked on the 23 black sts.
Continue straight for 15 rows.

First Shoulder
Armhole
On front side facing row, using black and beginning at the shoulder *knit 5, knit 2 together* repeat until 53 sts have been worked in black and the black meets the line of purple on the graph. (47)

Garter stitch for 8 rows. On the 9th row cast off 41 black sts leaving 6 at the underarm.

Higher Armhole
For a higher underarm than shown cast off only 36 black sts, work the next 6 sts in black garter and work the additional 10 sts not shown on the graph, in green.

Side slits
Continue underarm as established while working slit. At bottom edge on front facing row, knit last 26 sts in black. Continue in garter for 9 rows. Cast off all but 6 sts at top of slit. On next row cast on 20 black sts again. Garter stitch for 9 rows.

This completes the slit. Return to 6 sts of bottom band.

Armhole Continued
On the last garter stitch row cast on 41 sts for other side of armhole. Work 9 rows of black garter. Increase into every 7th stitch on last row of black. Continue straight on graph for 15 rows.

Back Neck Shaping
Work back neck shaping as graph. On a front facing row KNIT any stitch with another colour below it . On a wrong side facing row PURL any stitch with another colour below it. This will avoid bumps with crossed over colours.

Begin 1st row of back neck shaping by changing the first 7 pastel sts to 7 sts in black. Continue in black garter stitch for 9 rows while decreasing at the graph edge as shown. After 9 rows of black garter stitch cast off 8 black sts from the shoulder direction until 6 black sts remain.

Using 6 sts of black garter, work 32 rows straight or until 10 rows before last row of back shaping on graph. Cast on 8 black sts towards shoulder. Work increases at graph edge until 9 rows of black garter have been worked. Change these 7 sts to pastel and continue graph.

Third Shoulder Band
2nd Armhole
When back of neck is finished, work 15 rows straight from graph.

Armhole
On first row of black for second armhole *K2 tog, K5* to match other armhole. Work 9 rows black garter. Cast off and work remainder of armhole and side

slit to match first set.

Work 15 rows then begin the front neck reversing neck shaping.

Button Hole Band
Decrease to 78 sts. Work 10 rows in black garter stitch making 6 buttonholes (yarn over Knit 2 together) on a front facing middle row. Begin at neck edge as follows:
Knit 3, *yarn over, knit 2 tog, knit 10 * repeat from * to * 5 more times then complete row.

Embroidery
Using "roses" yarn and darning needle work a simple "over and over" stitch three times or so over any one stitch or row and in any direction. Move to next flower in a random fashion.

Sew shoulder seams.
Add buttons.

Begin Here
(Place buttonholes on this side if prefered)

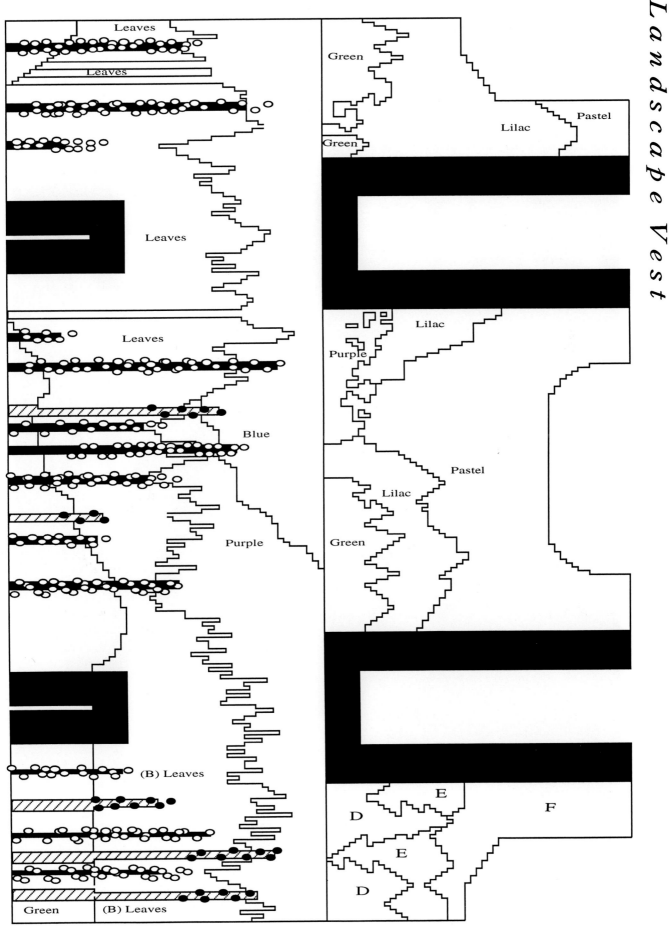

Seismograph

Technology reproduces the forces of nature as a line on paper. A line, by its nature divides one area from another and this in turn provides an opportunity for a colour change.

Plymouth Yarns Required
(100 gm balls)
(A) ENCORE #217 black x 3 (3, 3)
(B) ENCORE #174 claret x 4 (5, 5)

Needles

3^1/$_2$ mm (U.S. #4, U.K. #9 or #10)
for the bands and a circular
needle of the same size for the
neck band
4^1/$_2$ mm (U.S. #7 , U.K. #7)
for the body

Tension or Gauge

20 sts to 4" or 10 cm
27 rows to 4" or 10 cm

Garment Size

Width: 112 (119, 126) sts
= 22^1/$_2$" or 57 cm (23 ^{3}/$_4$"
or 60 cm, 25^1/$_2$" or 65 cm)
Length: repeat graph or any part
of graph as desired

Front

Using band needles and (B) cast
on 104 (110, 118) sts. Rib (K1, P1
every row) for 21 rows. On the
next purl row increase 8 or 9 sts
as required to 112 (119, 126) sts.
Change to body needles and
stocking stitch (Knit the front
facing rows and purl the back
facing rows.)

On a front facing row begin with
15 (20, 25) sts of (A) then tie a
thread to mark the first stitch of
the graph. Knit 7 sts with (A) for
the first 7 sts of the graph. Tie on
(B) and complete the 7 sts of the
graph row. Complete the row
in (B).

Continue with these two colours
following the graph until work
measures the required length.
Repeat the graph from the
beginning as necessary until 4"
(27 rows) from the desired
length. Put the 20 central stitches
on a holder. Work two together
at the neck edge each front facing
row five times. Continue straight

until required length. Cast off.
Work other shoulder to match.

Back

Work bands as front. Increase to
112 (119, 126) sts. Change to
body needles and stocking stitch.
Knit 82 (87, 92) sts in (B). Begin
graph. Read (A) for (B) and (B)
for (A). When work measures 1"
less than required length put the
central 20 sts on a holder. Work
2 tog at the neck edges each row
5 times. Work 2 rows straight.
Cast off shoulder.

Work other shoulder to match.

Left Sleeve

Cast on 50 sts using (A) and
work ribbing as for bands.
Change to body needles and
st st increase to 60 sts. Increase
one each edge every 6th row
until 80 (90, 100) sts. Continue
straight until sleeve is desired
length. Cast off loosely.

Right Sleeve

As left sleeve but use (B).

Neckband

Sew shoulder seams. With
circular needle pick up and knit
92 sts around neck hole. Rib 21
rows in (B). Cast off, sew seam,
fold in and stitch down.

Finishing

Sew sleeve seam and set sleeve
deeply into side seam. Sew
remaining side seams.

SPECIAL NOTE
It is not necessary to follow the
graph as provided. The concept
is more important than any
individual wiggle or zig zag.

The zig zag may even be worked
wider across the body or a
diagonal from shoulder to
shoulder.
Enjoy!

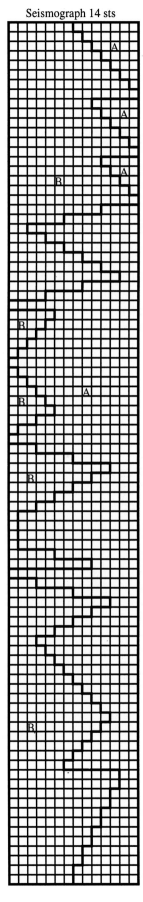

Seismograph 14 sts

Country Garden Vest

One of the greatest joys in life is a country garden. It rambles and changes from flower to flower but every year it returns. The eye enjoys both the order and the movement, the colour and the calm. This vest endeavours to capture that joy with multi-coloured painted yarns in repeating patterns that change by themselves.

Plymouth Yarns Required
All COTTON SOFT
(50 gm balls)
(A) #9005 roses x 1 (2, 2)
(B) #9003 leaves x 1 (2, 2)
(C) #9001 lilacs x 1 (2, 2)
(D) #9946 pastels x 1 (2, 2)
(E) #899 black x 3 (4, 4)

Needles
3 mm (U.S. #3 or U.K. #10) short circular, and long circular needles for bands
3.5 mm (U.S. #4 or U.K. #9) long circular or straight needles

Tension or Gauge
on Fairisle Body
(after pressing)
22 sts to 4" or 10 cm
22 rows to 4" or 10 cm

Garment Size
Child 7 to 13 years (as shown)
16" or 40 cm wide (180 sts)
17" or 43 cm long

Teen (not shown)
32" to 34" bust (192 sts)
21" or 53 cm long

Adult (not shown)
36" to 38" bust (216 sts)
21" or 53 cm long

Body
Do not begin with the band. Work all bands at the end so they match on the cast off edges.

Cast on 180 (192, 216) sts using black and body needles. Repeat the graph across the row. The row will not necessarily end with the graph. Begin the next row as necessary to maintain pattern. Continue graph until armhole row.

Teen and Adult
For teen and adult sizes work an extra row of black in-between each leaf or flower pattern to add approximately 4" or 10 cm in length. Add a total of 10 rows before the armhole and 10 rows after the armhole.

Underarm
Work 36 (38, 43), cast off 14 (16, 21) sts at the underarms, 80 (84, 88) on back, 14 (16, 21) for underarm, 36 (38, 43) on remaining front. Make three balls out of each colour and tie on new yarns at the back and front so complete rows can be worked at the same time if you wish. Work 2 tog at the armhole edges every front facing row until 30 (32, 37) remain on the each front and 68 (72, 76) remain on the back. Continue until the front neck shaping row.

Front Neck Shaping
Using back cast off 10 sts at the beginning of the first front leaving 26 (28, 33) and then again at end of the last front. Tie on the black again and continue. Work 2 together at the beginning of each front facing row at the neck edge until 17 (19, 24) sts remain.

Continue straight on all three sections until the back neck shaping row.

Back Neck Shaping
Knit 19 (21, 23) cast off 30 sts in the centre, knit 19 (21, 23). Work 2 together at the beginning of each front facing row at the neck edge until 17 (19, 21) sts remain. Continue straight on all three sections until the graph has been completed. Graft the shoulder seams together invisibly using black.

Press!

Fairisle Ribbed Band
Row 1: Using the band needle, black and facing the front, pick up and knit 181 (193, 217) stitches from the bottom edge.
Row 2: Wrong side facing row: Tie on "pastel". (Begin with a pastel stitch and end with a pastel stitch.)

*Purl 1 pastel. Knit 1 black * to end of row. P1 pastel.

If this is the first time you have done fairisle rib follows these hints: purl 1 pastel, keep pastel yarn on wrong side of work (your body side), put black to the right side (away from your body) knit the next stitch, bring the black back to the wrong side to carry behind. Always carry both colours on the wrong side of the work. Always carry both

Country Garden Vest

Country Garden Vest

 (A) ⬚ Roses

(B) ⬚ Leaves

(C) ⬚ Lilac

(D) ⬚ Pastels

(E) ☐ Black

X Work stitch in
reverse stocking
stitch to make
bump.

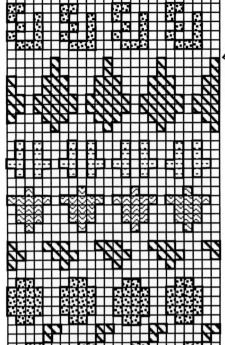

Back neck shaping row

Knit 2 tog at neck edge.
Cast off 10 sts at neck edge,
for front shaping

Armhole Row

Armhole Ribbing
Using short band circular needles pick up and knit on front facing side 112 (122, 132) sts. Alternate one st in pastel and one in black. Work as for bottom band for next 3 rows. Cast off tightly ribwise using "lilacs" (C).

Neckband Ribbing
Pick up and knit 105 sts on front facing side. Alternate one st in pastel and one in black. Begin and end with a black stitch. Work as for bottom band (more firmly every row) until only one row has been worked in "leaves" (B). Cast off VERY tightly on smaller needle ribwise using "lilacs" (C).

Front Button Band Ribbing
Pick up knitwise on front facing side 81 (91, 101) sts. Alternate one st in pastel and one in black. Begin and end with a "pastel" stitch. Work as for neck band. Cast off tightly in rib using "lilacs" (C).

Front Button Hole Band Ribbing
Match pickup row EXACTLY to the other front. On the last pastel row make button holes as follows:
Rib 3, *cast off 2, rib 10 (11, 12) *, repeat from * to * to make 7 buttonholes altogether, end with rib 4.

colours to the end of the row and twist them before starting the next row.

Row 3: Cut black and lay in or tie on "roses" (A). Work as above but make roses the dip stitch or purl stitch on the right facing side. *K1 pastel, P 1 roses* End K1 pastel. P1 pastel.

Row 4: *P1 pastel, K1 roses*
Row 5: Cut pastel and replace

with "lilacs" (C). Continue as established.

Row 6: as established.
Row 7: Cut "roses" (A) and replace with "leaves" (B).

Row 8: as established
Row 9: as established

Row 10: Cut leaves and cast off firmly rib wise with "lilacs" (C). Sew shoulder seams

Next row: replace the missing two stitches by making an "e" cast on in each colour above the cast off sts.
Continue until band matches other front. Cast off tightly ribwise using "lilacs" (C).

Finishing
Press again very well stretching the fairisle body. Sew on seven buttons. Check inside for tails and sew in along own colour.

Pyramid Tunic

This red tunic with dramatic diagonal and diamond patterns is ideal for the fuller figure. Instructions are included for a smaller, shorter pullover and a narrower tunic.

Plymouth Yarns Required
(100 gm hanks)
(A) GALWAY #09 black x 2
(B) GALWAY #24 purple x 3
(C) GALWAY # 16 red x 5 (6, 6)
(D) GALWAY # 18 teal x 2
(E) GALWAY # 23 cerise x 1

Needles
4 mm (U.S. #6, U.K. #8) for
bands and circular needle for
the neckband
4¹/₂ mm (U.S. #7, U.K. #7)

Tension or Gauge
20 sts to 4" or 10 cm
26 rows to 4" or 10 cm

Instructions for the standard
pullover are first, instructions for
a standard tunic are first inside
the bracket and the instructions
for the fuller figured tunic (as
shown in the photograph) are
second inside the brackets.
Unless specified all remaining
instructions apply to all shapes
and sizes.

Garment Size
Width: 99 (119, 139) sts = 20" or
51 cm (24" or 61 cm, 28" or 71 cm)
Graph rows: 140 (200, 200)
Length with bands: 24¹/₂" or
63 cm (31" or 79 cm)

Back
Cast on 90 (100,120) sts in black.
Rib for 20 rows for pullover.
Both tunic bands: use body size
needles. Stocking stitch for one
inch (knit front facing row and
purl back facing rows). Work one
row in reverse stocking stitch to

Pyramid Tunic

make a turn row. Work one inch in stocking stitch.

Increase to 99 (119, 139) sts in black on a purl row. Change to body needles. Begin graph.

Back Neck Shaping

At 135 (195, 195) graph rows put the central 19 sts on a holder and work two sts together at each neck edge each row five times. Cast off. Work other shoulder to match.

Front

Work as for back for 110 (170, 170) graph rows. Put the central 19 sts on a holder. Complete row. Work two sts together at each neck edge each front facing row five times till same number of sts as shoulder of back.

Continue straight till length matches back. Cast off. Work other shoulder to match.

Sleeves

Cast on 35 (40, 46) sts. Work as for bottom band. Change to body needles. Increase to 45 (51, 59) sts. Use centre of the graph. Increase one each edge every 6th row. After triangles have been worked at the bottom and the red introduced, continue in the red until 1" short of the desired length. Work one inch in black stocking stitch. Leave off the black line at the top of the sleeves if a slimmer line is desired. Cast off loosely.

Neckband

Sew shoulder seams. Using black pick up and knit 77 sts. Work as for bottom band. Cast off loosely. Fold inside and stitch down.

Sew sleeves in deeply. Sew tails and finishing hemming bottom of tunic. Press gently.

Adjust length here

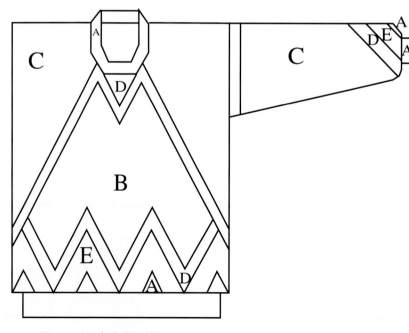

Pyramid Pullover

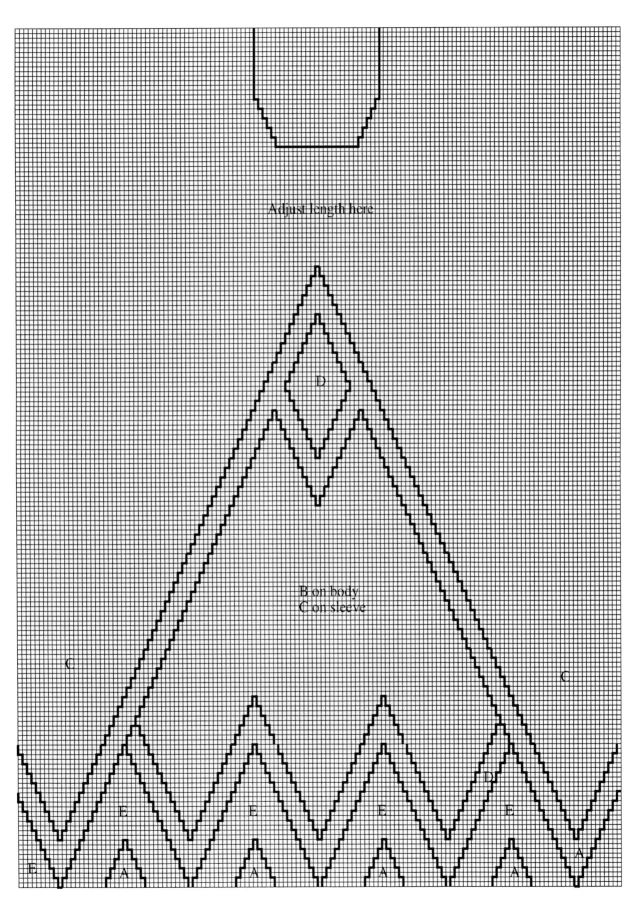

Adjust length here

D

B on body
C on sleeve

C

C

E

E

E

E

E

E

A

A

A

A

A

D

Scottie Dog

This perky variation on a traditional tartan and Scottie dog sweater can be worked as a pullover (as shown) or as a larger tunic. Instructions for the tunic are given in brackets.

Pyramid Yarns Required
(A) GALWAY #16 red x 2 (2)
(B) GALWAY #09 black x 1 (2)
(C) GALWAY #11 blue x 1 (2)
(D) GALWAY #45 green x 1 (2)
(E) GALWAY #24 purple x 1 (2)
(F) GALWAY #18 teal x 1 (2)
(G) GALWAY #60 yellow x 1 (1)
(H) GALWAY #8 white x 1 (1)

Needles
3$^{1}/_{2}$ mm (U.S. #4, U.K. #9 or #10) for the bands and a circular needle of the same size for the neck band
4$^{1}/_{2}$ mm (U.S. #7, U.K. #7) for the body

Tension or Gauge
20 sts and 26 rows to 4" or 10 cm

Garment Size
Pullover
Width: 100 sts = 20" or 50 cm
Length: 120 rows of graph = 18$^{1}/_{2}$" or 47 cm plus 3" band = 21$^{1}/_{2}$" or 55 cm

Tunic
Width: 120 sts = 61 cm or 24" or 62 cm
Length: 160 rows of graph = 24$^{1}/_{2}$" plus 2$^{1}/_{2}$" band = 27" or 79 cm

Textured Stitch
Row 1: K1, P1
Row 2: P1, K1
Row 3: P1, K1
Row 4: P1, K1
Repeat these 4 rows.

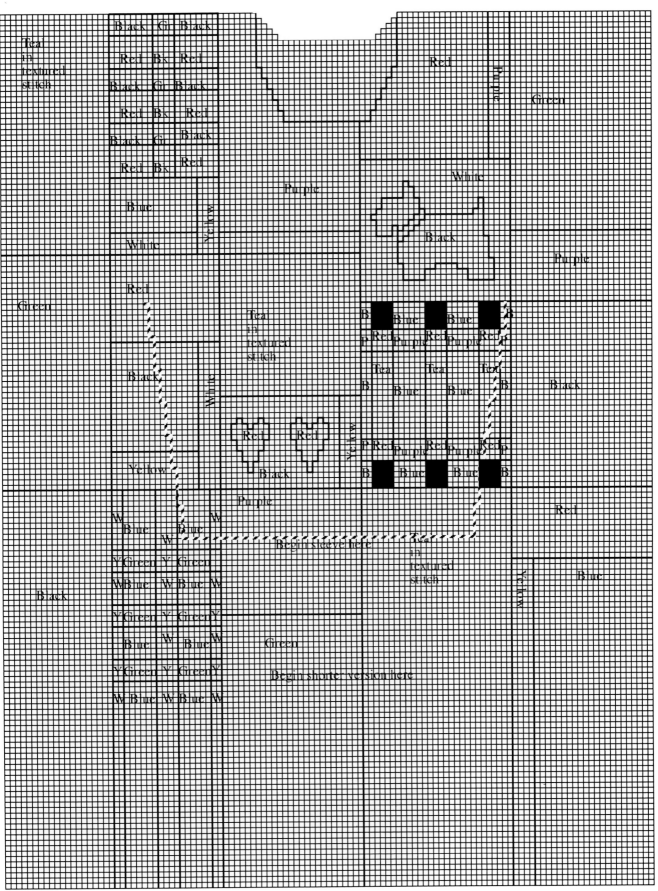

Front

Using band needles and red cast on 90 (110) sts. Work textured stitch for 3" (2$^1/_2$"). On the next purl row increase 10 sts to 100 (120) sts. Change to body needles and stocking stitch (Knit the front facing rows and purl the back facing rows.)

On a front facing row begin the graph. Leave off the outside 10 sts and the bottom 40 rows for the pullover. Work the full graph for the tunic. Continue until 20 rows from the end. Put the 18 central stitches on a holder. Work two together at the neck edges each front facing row five times. Continue straight for 10 rows. Cast off. Work other shoulder to match.

Back

Work as for front until 5 rows from the end. Begin back neck shaping. Put the central 18 sts on a holder. Work 2 tog at the neck edges on each row 5 times. Cast off shoulder. Work other shoulder to match.

Sleeve

Cast on 48 sts using red and work as for bottom bands. Change to body needles and increase to 54 sts. Use the centre 54 sts of the body graph as shown. Increase one each edge on each 6th row until desired length. The tunic will have a shorter sleeve as the body is wider. Cast off loosely.

Neckband

Sew shoulder seams. Pick up and knit 86 sts in red around neck hole and work as for bottom band. Cast off, sew seam, fold in and stitch down.

Swiss darn red collar on dog as shown on graph. Set sleeves in armhole deeply at 5 sts to 8 rows. Put away all tails and press gently.

Yes, we know the dog isn't a Scottie, but he volunteered during the photo shoot!

Flags

Red flags repeat on the green in this playful multicolour design with simple textures. Black and white borders provide a moment of relief before play begins again.

Plymouth Yarns Required
All COTTON SOFT 50 gm balls unless specified

(A)   #339 apricot x 1
(Black) #899 black x 1
(CB) #034 cerulean blue x 1
(B)   #247 blue x 1
(G)   #536 kelly green x 1
(HP) # 319 hot pink x 1
(J)   #269 jade x 1
(L)   ENCORE #215 lemon x 1
(LG) #548 light green x 1
(M) #616 magenta x 1
(P)   #628 purple x 1
(R)   #361 red x 1
(RB) #255 royal blue x 2
(S)   #025 sky blue x 1
(T)   ENCORE #473 teal mix x 1
(W) #800 white x 1
(WB)#631 wedgewood blue x 1
(Y) # 709 yellow x 1

Photocopy colour list and attach a small strand of each colour before taking paper bands off the balls.

Needles
4 mm (U.S. #6, U.K. #8) for bands
Circular needles as above
4¹/₂ mm (U.S. #7, U.K. #7) for body or as required to achieve tension

Tension or Gauge
20 sts to 4" or 10 cm
26 rows to 4" or 10 cm

Garment Size
Small (Medium/Large)
Width: 100 (110, 120) sts
20" or 51 cm (22" or 56 cm, 24"or 61 cm)
Length: 130 (140, 150) graph rows plus 25 rows band.

23" or 59 cm (24" or 62 cm, 25" or 64 cm)

Back
Cast on 90 (100, 110) sts using band needles and rib for 25 rows using (RB). Change to body needles and stocking stitch. Increase evenly to 100 (110, 120) sts. Ignore the bottom 20 (10, 0) rows of graph and the outside 10 (5, 0) sts on each side. Complete graph using a knit stitch on the purl row or a purl stitch on the knit row when the unit is marked with a "x".
Cast off back straight and loose.

Front
As back but shape the neck 28 rows from the end. Put the central 10 sts on a holder and decrease one each side as graph. Continue straight for 22 rows. Cast off loosely.

Sleeve
Using (RB) and band needles, cast on 36 (40, 44) sts and rib for 25 rows. Increase to 56, change to body needles and st st and begin the graph. Increase one each side every 6th row till end of graph or desired length. Work unmarked block of colours using any favorite colour combinations in remaining yarns. Do not make both sleeves the same. For more length repeat final 18 rows using any desired colours.

Cast off loosely.

Neckband
Sew shoulder seams. Using (WB) with front side facing, and circular needles pick up and knit 14 sts down one front, 8 on the decreases, 10 from the holder, 8, then 14 sts and then 22 across the back of the neck (76 sts). Rib for 22 rows and cast off loosely. Fold out and sew down.

Finishing
Sew the sleeve seams. Sew the side seams up to but not including the black bar on the right. Set sleeve deeply. Sew remaining tails and press gently.

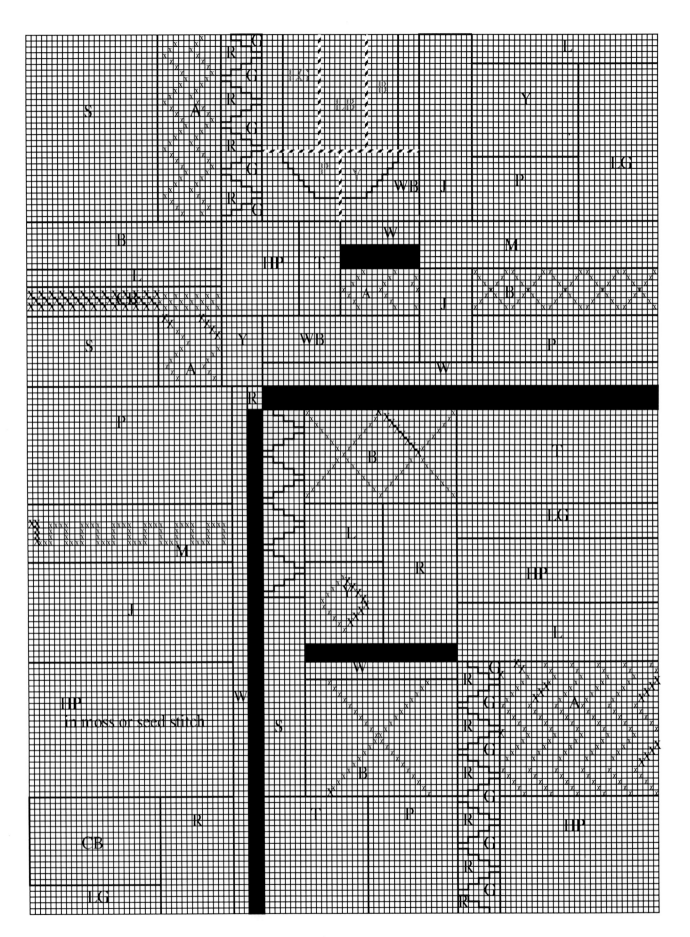

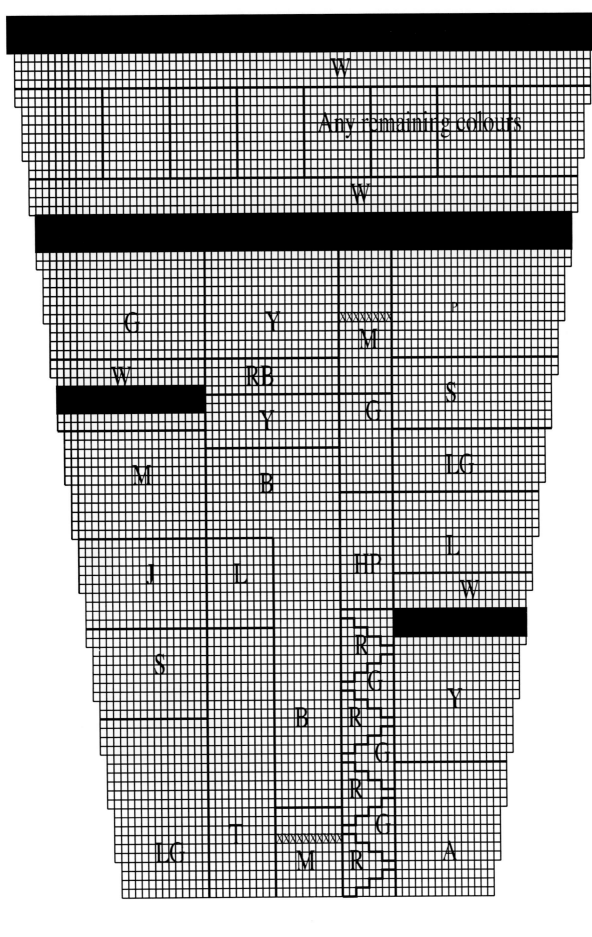

Sunset at Sea

This fun loving, fresh design is the story of the sea. It begins at the bottom with green seaweed. The eye travels up the sweater through layers of fish and bubbles until waves, outlined in blue embroidery, break the surface to a multi - coloured sky. The yoke is a bright sunset with floating white clouds. One sleeve has green star fish and lilac shells, the other has coral and sea horses.

Plymouth Yarns Required

All COTTON SOFT unless otherwise specified (50 gm balls)
(A) #800 white x 2
(B) ENCORE # 215 lemon x 1
(C) #709 yellow x 1
(D) #319 pink x 1
(E) #631 lilac x 1
(F) #638 purple x 1
(G) #339 orange x 1
(H) #247 wedgewood blue x 1
(J) #255 royal blue x 1
(K) #263 navy blue x 1
(L) #025 light blue x 1
(P) #034 deep cerulean blue x 2
(Q) #548 light green x 1
(R) #361 red x 1
(S) #899 black x 1
(T) #060 dark jade x 2
(W) #057 forest green x 1

Photocopy the list of colors and attach a small strand of each color before taking the bands off the balls of yarn.

Needles

Circular needles are recommended because this cardigan has a lot of stitch. Turn and work as if on straight needles.

Bands 4.5 mm (U.S. #7, U.K. #6 or #7)
Body 5.5 mm (U.S. #10, U.K. #5)

Tension or Gauge

Fairisle rib = 20 sts and 28 rows to 4" or 10 cm
Fairisle body = 17 sts and 20 rows to 4" or 10 cm

Garment Size

Width: 23$\frac{1}{2}$" or 60 cm
Length: 27$\frac{1}{2}$" or 70 cm

* * = Repeat between * and *.

Body Band

Always carry both colours behind, to the end and twist. Begin with the fairisle ribbed band using band needles and black (S) cast on 182 sts.

Row 1, 3 and 5: (front facing rows) Knit 2 blue (J), purl 2 black across row.
Row 2, 4 and 6: Knit 2 black, Purl 2 blue across row.

Row 7: Cut off blue, tie on purple (F). Work 6 rows as established replacing the blue with the purple.

Row 13: Cut off purple tie on jade (T). Work 6 rows as established replacing the purple with the green.

Body

Increase 1 every 12th stitch to 198 sts. Change to body needles. Begin working from body graph. All rows to armhole are 9 stitch repeats worked 22 times. Work in stocking stitch (knit front facing rows and purl back

facing rows). Weave in tails fairisle fashion at the back of the work or later as desired. Carry no more than two stitches at the back. Carry LOOSELY.
Row 59: Work in all black (S).
Row 60: all black
Leave on holder and begin "Starfish Sleeve."

Starfish Sleeve

Using red (R) and band needles cast on 36 sts. Tie on yellow (C).
Row 1: K2 yellow, P2 red across the row. Always carry both colours to the end of the row and twist at the end.
Row 2: (wrong side facing) K2 red, P2 yellow across the row. Continue for a total of six rows of fairisle rib.
Row 7: Cut yellow, tie on orange (G). As above replacing yellow with orange. Work six rows.
Row 13: Cut orange, tie on pink. As above replacing orange with pink. Work six rows.

Change to body needles and stocking stitch, cut red and tie on jade (T) and increases 9 sts across the row (45). Use starfish graph.

Continue on T and 79 sts until sleeve measures desired length.

Right side facing: Cast off the first 7 sts loosely, work 66 sts, cast off the last 6 stitches. Leave stitches on a holder.

Sea Horse Sleeve

Work cuff as first sleeve. Change to body needles and stocking stitch. Increase to 45 sts. Work from seahorse graph.

Continue in blue (P) on 79 sts until desired length.
Cast off first 6 sts, work 66 sts, cast off last 7 stitches.

Armholes

In black, K42 for front, cast off 15

Sunset at Sea Graphs

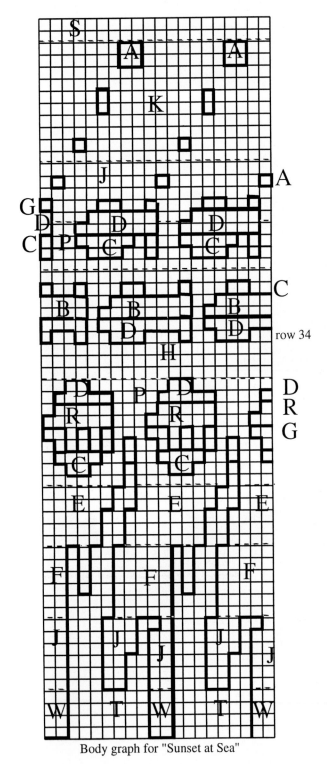

Body graph for "Sunset at Sea"

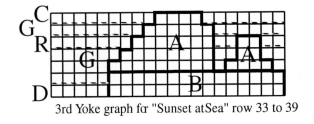

3rd Yoke graph for "Sunset at Sea" row 33 to 39

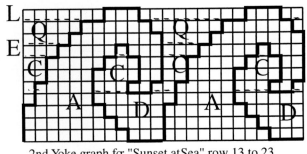

2nd Yoke graph for "Sunset at Sea" row 13 to 23

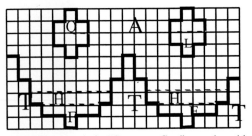

1st Yoke graph for "Sunset at Sea" row 1 to 11

sts from the body for armhole, knit 84 sts for back, cast off 15 sts for armhole, K42 sts for other front.

This next section collects all the stitches from the body and the sleeves to do the yoke. More importantly, it also lengthens the back to make the neck of the garment fit better.

Transfer Row

In black knit 42 sts from front, K66 stitches from "starfish sleeve". Tie on (T) to the black yarn, K84 stitches from back in (T). Turn work and purl 84

stitches in (T), turn work.

Continue over these 84 stitches until 6 rows have been worked. Cut (T).

Continue in black, knitting the 84 stitches from the back then the 66 stitches from the "sea horse sleeve" and the remaining 42 from the last front. (300 sts.)

Yoke

Row 1: The graph shows 20 sts but it is a 10 stitch repeat. Tie on (T) and (F). Begin the 1st yoke graph working the 10 stitch repeat 30 times.

Row 11: work one row in white.
Row 12: (1st decrease row in yoke) Work all in white. K3,* K2 together (tog), K4,* to centre back, K6 without decreasing. Continue *K2 tog, K4,* K3 (252 stitches).

Row 13: Begin second yoke graph of a wave. The graph shows 24 sts but it is a 12 stitch repeat. Work the 12 stitch repeat 21 times. Tie on pink (D). *K3 pink, K9 white*

Row 24: Cut white and work the 2nd decrease row in light blue (L). K1,* K3, K2 tog* K3. Count

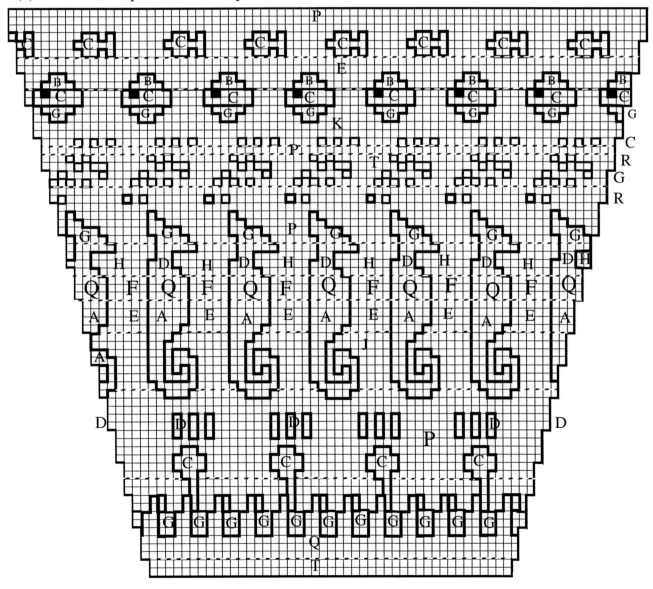

stitches.

Row 25: Work 1 row in light blue (L) adjusting to 200 stitches as necessary.

Row 26: Cut light blue, tie on (P). Knit one row.

Row 27: Purl in (P).

Row 28: Cut (P), tie on blue (H). K one row.

Row 29: Cut (H), tie on lilac (E). K one row.

Row 30: All lilac

Row 31: Cut lilac, tie on pink (D). K one row

Row 32: Decrease row in pink. *K8, K2 tog* (180 sts)

Begin third yoke graph

Row 33: Tie on lemon. *K15 lemon (B) , K5 pink (D)*

Row 40: Cut yellow (C) and white (A), tie on lemon (B). Work decrease row all in lemon. *K2 tog, K8* (162 sts)

Row 41 and 42: Purl in lemon

Row 43: Cut lemon, tie on light green (Q). Decrease row *K4, K2 tog* (135 sts)

Row 44: Cut light green (Q), tie on light blue (L). Purl one row.

Row 45: Decrease in light blue (L), K2 tog *K2, K2 tog*

Row 46: Purl one row in light blue adjusting to 100 sts.

Row 47: Decrease in light blue (L),

K3, K2 tog (80 sts)

Row 48: Purl one row in light blue

Neckband

Using band needles.

Row 1: Right side facing. Tie on yellow (C) K1 yellow, *K2 blue, K2 yellow* K2 blue, K1 yellow.

Row 2: P1 yellow, * K2 blue, P 2 yellow* K2 blue, P 1 yellow.

Row 3: K1 yellow,* P2 blue, K2 yellow,* P2 blue, K1 yellow.

Row 4: as row 2

Row 5: Cut yellow, tie on pink. Cut blue and tie on light green.

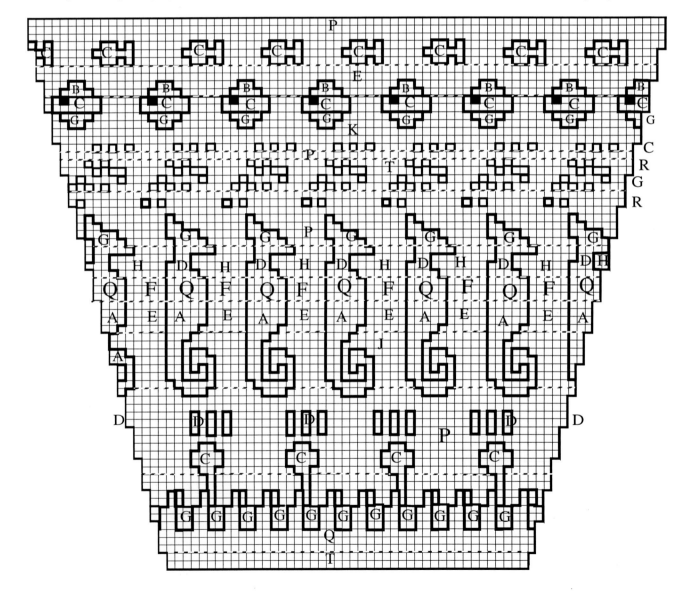

Continue as established for 4 rows.
Row 9: Cut light green, and pink, tie on lilac (E). Knit one row with right side facing.
Row 10: KNIT in lilac
Row 11: Cut lilac, tie on (P). KNIT one row.
Row 12: Cast off in (P), knitwise.

Front bands

Using red and a very fine hard knitting needle of any small gauge, pick up the stitches for the front band. Begin from bottom ribbing end with front side facing as follows: 11 sts from the ribbing, then 1 every 2nd row. (70 sts). Do not pick up from 2 rows of garter stitch at top of neck. Knit a row (wrong side facing) in red adjusting to 70 sts as necessary.

Row 1: (right side facing) Cut orange, tie on light blue (L) and yellow (C). *K2 light blue, K2 yellow into the next red stitch,* K1 light blue (23 sets of yellow)
Row 2: K1 light blue,* P2 yellow, K2 light blue*
Row 3: right side facing *P2 light blue, K2 yellow,* P1 light blue
Row 4: as row 2

Button Hole Row

Row 5: Button hole row. Cut light blue, tie on light green (Q).

Right side facing row: P2 green, K2 yellow, P2 green, K1 yellow, slip next yellow stitch onto right hand needle, cast off one blue stitch over the top of the other on the row below, slip yellow stitch back onto left hand needle, knit the yellow stitch and the remaining blue stitch together through the BACK of the stitches.

Rebuild the two missing stitches as follows: twist the yellow and green yarns around each other, wrap the green over the right hand needle, twist the yellow and green yarn around each other again, wrap the green over the right hand needle, twist the yellow and green around each other again. K2 yellow, P2 green, K2 yellow, P2 green, K2 yellow, P2 green, K1 yellow. Make next button hole.

There should be three green sets and four yellow sets in-between each button hole and a total of 6 button holes. End row with K2 yellow.

Row 6: P2 together with yellow at neck edge to begin forming the curve. P1 yellow, *K2 green, P2 yellow,* K2 green
Row 7: right side facing. Cut yellow, tie on pink. *P2 green, K2 pink* P2 green, K2 tog with pink.
Row 8: Cut pink, tie on lilac. K2 tog with green, K1 green, *P2 lilac, K2 green*
Row 9: Cut lilac and green, tie on red. Knit one row, K last 2 sts tog. Pick up 6 sts around top curve plus 1 from the 1st row of red at beginning of band.
Row 10: Knit in red.
Row 11: Leave red attached, tie on deep cerulean blue (P). Knit one row and pick up one stitch from the cast off row of (P) on the neckband.
Row 12: Cast off knitwise facing the wrong side in (P). Leave ball attached.

Finish the bottom of the band as follows:
Wrong side facing: Using red pick up 4 sts purlwise, plus 1 from the red. Turn work. Purl row in red. Cut red leaving 5" tail. Purl one row in blue, pick up 1 from cast on row of body. Turn work. Cast off purlwise in blue.

Sew red corner then blue corner firmly with tails.

Button Band

Work second front band with out button holes. Take special care when picking up the red and again on row 1. Match the blue and yellow stripes to the exact position on the other front so the designs in the body and the button and button holes line up.
Finish the garter in purl rather than knit to match other front.

Embroidery

On Sea Horse Sleeve embroider a line in stem stitch using lemon between the white and the light green on the sea horse.

On Starfish Sleeve embroider a tail and eye on the fish using yellow. Work 4 satin stitches in fan shape for a tail on each fish and over a single stitch a couple of times for the eye.

On body embroider a tail and eye on the 1st layer of fish using yellow.

On yoke embroider the wave using a couching technique as follows: Lay a blue (H) line around the white wave and then stitch it in place.

Finishing

Sew cuffs from outside using red. Reinforce at beginning then sew catching the red wrapped stitch at the end of the row on the multicoloured side and the last red purl stitch on the red side. Reinforce at the top of the cuff. Change to cerulean blue. Sew remaining sleeve with this colour or ideally match the colours using the tails. Reinforce at top of sleeve. Sew underarm using black or navy easing the differences. Sew on Paua shell or abalone buttons. Check inside for tails and sew in along own colour.

Shadow Tiles

Black, charcoal, and grey in Plymouth Encore graduate up the sweater in a dramatic triangular pattern.

Plymouth Yarns Required
(100 gm balls)
(A) ENCORE #240 taupe x 1
(B) ENCORE #217 black x 3
(C) GALWAY #3 beige x 1
(D) ENCORE #389 charcoal x 2
(E) ENCORE #208 white x 1

Needles
$3^1/_2$ mm (U.S. #4, U.K. #9 or #10) for the bands
Circular needle as above
$4^1/_2$ mm (U.S. #7, U.K. #7) for the body

Tension or Gauge
20 sts to 4" or 10 cm
26 rows to 4" or 10 cm

Garment Size
Width: 121 sts = $23^3/_4$" or 60 cm
Length: 160 rows of graph plus 3" bands = $27^1/_2$" or 70 cm

Back
Using band needles and black cast on (100) sts. Rib 3".

On the next purl row increase to (120) sts. Change to body needles and stocking stitch (knit the front facing rows and purl the back facing rows).

Begin the graph, tie on separate balls of yarn for each colour. Take special care on the first row.

Keep the yarn 'cross overs' at the

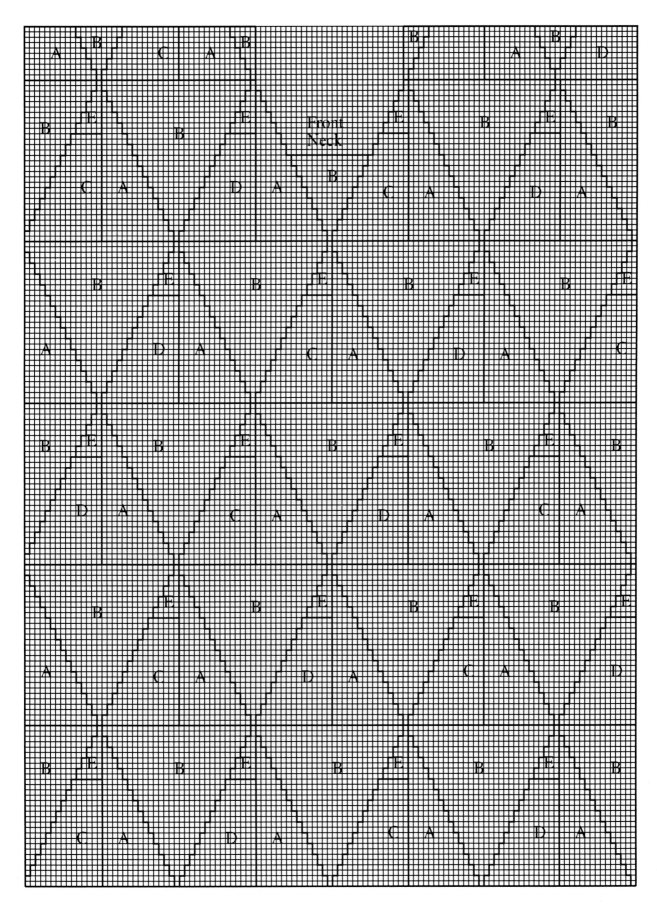

colour changes firm and tight. Work final stitch as first stitch on right side of graph. Continue working until 5 rows from the end.

Neck Hole
Put 21 central sts on holder. Work 2 tog at the neck edge every row 5 times. Cast off shoulder. Work other shoulder to match.

Front
As back until 30 rows from the end.
For neck (as photographed) put 21 central sts on holder. For neater, narrower neck (as graph) put the 17 central stitches on a holder. Work two together at the neck edge each front facing row 5 times (7).
Continue straight until front matches the back. Cast off remaining 46 sts.

Sleeves
Cast on 52 sts and rib for 3". Change to body needles and increase to 61 sts. Use centre 61 sts of body graph. Increase one each edge every 6th row thereafter until long enough, ending at one of the natural breaks.

Cast off loosely.

Neckband
Sew shoulder seams. Using circular needles pick up and knit 92 sts around neck hole, rib for 3". Cast off, fold in and stitch down.

Four Sheep and a Camel

This is a simple variation on Shadow Tiles in black, charcoal, and grey in Encore. Named Four Sheep and a Camel because the charcoal or 'black sheep' triangle appears four times and the camel coloured triangle appears once.

Plymouth Yarns Required
(100 gm balls)
(A) ENCORE #240 taupe x 1
(B) ENCORE # 217 black x 4
(C) GALWAY #3 beige x 1
(D) ENCORE #389 charcoal x 1
(E) ENCORE # 208 white x 1

Needles
$3^1/_2$ mm (U.S. #5, U.K. #9)
for the bands
Circular needle as above
$4^1/_2$ mm (U.S. #7, U.K. #7)
for the body

Tension or Gauge
20 sts to 4" or 10 cm
26 rows to 4" or 10 cm

Width: 90 (100, 110) sts = 20 (22, 24), 51 cm (56, 60 cm)
Length: 160 rows of graph plus 3" bands = $27^1/_2$" or 70 cm

Back

Using band needles and black cast on 90 (100, 110) sts. Rib 3"

On the next purl row increase to 100 (110, 120) sts. Change to body needles and stocking stitch (Knit the front facing rows and purl the back facing rows.)

Begin the graph. Work first 30 sts only. Work remainder of row in black. Complete first 30 rows and first full charcoal triangle set. Row 31: work 16 sts in black, work second camel triangle (30 sts). Work remainder of row in black. Complete 2nd triangle set as established. Continue using the "charcoal" triangle set only and moving the position every 30 rows as established.

Continue working until 5 rows from the end. Put 20 central sts on holder. Work 2 tog at the neck edge on every row 5 times. Cast off 46 shoulder stitches. Work other shoulder to match.

Front

As back until 30 rows from the end. Put the 20 central stitches on a holder. Work two together at the neck edges each front facing row five times. Continue straight until front matches the back. Cast off 46 shoulder stitches.

Sleeves

Cast on 43 (47, 51) sts and rib for 3". Change to body needles and st st. Increase to 53, (57, 61) sts. Use centre sts of body graph. Increase one each edge every 6th row until long enough. Cast off loosely. Or work sleeves all black.

Neckband

Sew shoulder seams. Using circular needles pick up and knit 92 around neck hole. Rib for 3". Cast off, fold to inside and stitch down.

Four Sheep and a Camel

Earth Energy

Uplifting waves of deep rich earth colours zig zag across this warm sweater in machine washable Plymouth Encore used double throughout. The combination of two yarns allows this coat to adapt easily to different gauges to make three different sizes. Use large needle sizes for a casual oversized cardigan, or smaller needles for a firmer, more formal jacket.

Plymouth Yarns Required

(100 gm balls) for both sizes
(A) ENCORE #217 black x 4
(B) ENCORE #174 cranberry x 4
(C) ENCORE #504 egg plant x 2
(D) ENCORE #044 blue thunder x 2
(E) ENCORE #473 teal mix x 3
(F) ENCORE #223 brown x 2

5 buttons

Small/Medium

Needles
4 mm (U.S. #5 or #6, U.K. #8)
for the bands
5.5 mm (U.S. #10, U.K. #4)
for the body

Tension or Gauge
15.5 sts to 4" or 10 cm
18 rows to 4" or 10 cm

Garment Size
Width: 90 sts = 27^1/$_2$" or 70 cm
Length: 140 rows of graph plus
2" band = 33" or 84 cm

Medium/Large

Needles
5 mm (U.S. #9, U.K. #5) for
the bands
6.5 mm (U.S. #10½, U.K. #3)
for the body

Tension or Gauge
14 sts to 4" or 10 cm
17 rows to 4" or 10 cm

Garment Size
Width: 90 sts = 26" or 66 cm
Length: 140 rows of graph plus
2" band = 36" or 91 cm

Large/Extra Large
(extra yarn may be required)

Needles
5.5 mm (U.S. #10, U.K. #4)
for the bands
7.5 mm (U.S. #11, U.K. #1)
for the body

Tension or Gauge
12.5 sts to 4" or 10 cm
16 rows to 4" or 10 cm

Garment Size
Width: 90 sts = 29" or 74 cm
Length: 140 rows of graph plus
2" band = 38" or 97 cm

Back
Using band needles and (A)
DOUBLED cast on 80 sts.
Work band pattern as follows:

Band Pattern
Row 1 to 4 - (K1, P1 across row).
Row 5 to 8 - (P1, K1 across row).
Row 9 to 11 - as row 1 to 4.

On the next wrong side facing
row, increase in purl to 90 sts.
Change to body needles and
stocking stitch (knit the front
facing rows and purl the back
facing rows.)

On a front facing row begin the

graph. Continue straight until back neck shaping (5 rows from end). Put the central 12 sts on a holder. Work 2 tog at the neck edge 5 times. Cast off remaining 34 sts for shoulder. Work other shoulder to match.

Front

Work front body and band at the same time. The front band has 8 sts of stocking stitch which folds inside to form a stable front button band.

Cast on 52 sts in (A). Work bottom band pattern as follows:

Row 1: Work 44 sts in band pattern and final 8 sts in knit.
Row 2: Purl 8, band pattern 44 sts.

Continue as established keeping the outside 8 sts in stocking stitch for a total of 11 rows.

On next wrong side facing row, increase as follows:

Purl 8, work band pattern for 8 sts, purl the rest of the row increasing 4 sts evenly across the row (8 for front facing, 8 for front band pattern, 40 for graph sts = 56 sts).

Work the outside 40 sts of the graph in stocking stitch while maintaining the band pattern and facing as established and using colours as identified in the graph. Use a stitch marker to maintain the division between the band pattern and body.

Note: For a neat colour transition in the button and buttonhole bands, work the colour change row all in stocking stitch. On the following row go back to the pattern as it would be had the stocking stitch row been a normal pattern row.

Important

Since the band pattern is longer than stocking stitch, MISS every 9th and 10 rows of the front band, this will make the band 20 rows less than the body and the correct gauge to match the stocking stitch body.

Pocket Edging

After 30 rows work the outside 4 sts in band pattern for 20 rows to form the pocket edging. Return to all st st. Continue straight till 25 rows from the end.

Neckhole

Cast off the 8 facing stitches, work the 8 band pattern sts and 4 body sts and then place them on a holder. Work two together at the neck edge each front facing row until 34 sts remain. Continue straight until front matches the back.

Front with Buttonhole Band

Reverse instructions for other front but also add buttonholes as follows:

Work button holes in pairs, placing one button hole in the facing and another on the same row in the front band.

Begin 1st buttonhole on row 7 of graph and every 22nd row (of band not graph) thereafter.

Work buttonhole on stitch 3 of band facing, and again on stitch 5 of band pattern.

Stitch 5 should be a purl stitch. P1, K1, P1, K1, yarn to front (this will form a yarn over), K2 together, P1, K1.
The final buttonhole is worked in the neckband.

Sleeve

Using band needles and (A) cast on 38 sts. Work band pattern for 11 rows. Change to body needles and stocking stitch. Increase to 46 sts evenly spaced across row. Increase one each edge every 4th row while working the graph or the desired length. Cast off loosely. Work second sleeve to match.

Neckband

Sew shoulder seams. With front side facing and band needle, knit up the 12 front sts on the holder, pick up 16 from neck diagonal, 20 from back of neck, 16 from other diagonal and 12 from the last holder (total 76 sts) in (B).

Work band pattern for 12 rows working a buttonhole 22 rows after last buttonhole.

Inside Neck Band

Stocking stitch for the final 11 rows working a matching buttonhole as required. Cast off and fold in and stitch down.

Pocket Linings

Sew side seams leaving 12" or 30 cm for sleeve hole and leaving the 20 row pocket edging open.

Cast on 20 st in (F) single or double as desired and st st for 30 rows. Cast off. Sew cast off edge to inside front in line with the top of the pocket edging.

Sew side of pocket to side seam of back. Sew remaining two sides to inside front with the bottom of the pocket 10 rows or more below the pocket edging.

Finishing

Fold in the facings. Stitch around buttonholes matching holes in facing. Sew on buttons.

Sew sleeve seams. Set sleeves deeply. Press gently.

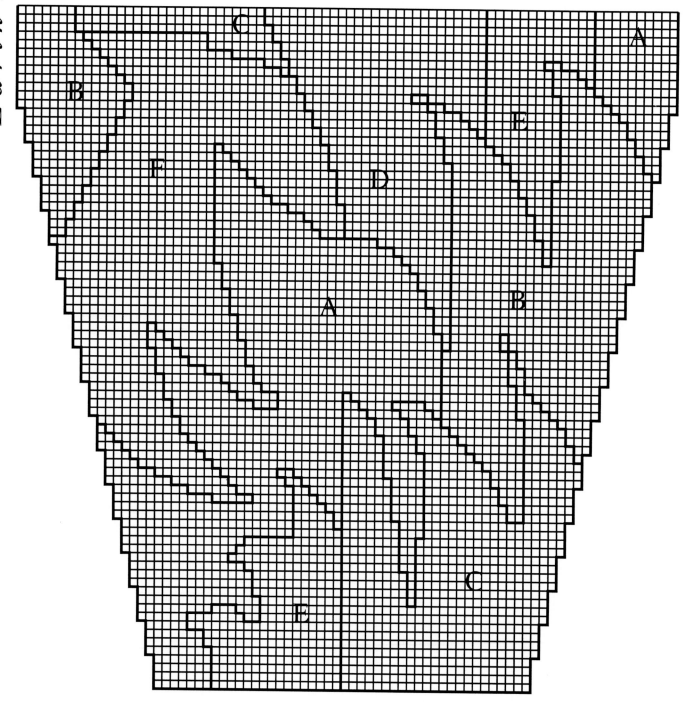

Optics

Fresh colours and a machine washable yarn combine into a fun, adaptable statement.

Plymouth Yarns Required
(100 gm balls)
(A) ENCORE #215 lemon x 1 (1, 1)
(B) ENCORE #194 grey heather x 2 (3, 3)
(C) ENCORE #9403 med blue x 2 (3, 3)
(D) ENCORE #208 white x 2 (3, 3)
(E) ENCORE #217 black x 2 (3, 3)

Needles
$3^1/_2$ mm (U.S. #4, U.K. #9 or 10) for the bands
Circular needles as above
$4^1/_2$ mm (U.S. #7 or #8, U.K. #7) for the body

Tension or Gauge
20 sts to 4" or 10 cm
26 rows to 4" or 10 cm

Width: 100 (110, 120) sts = 20" (22" or 56 cm, 24" or 61 cm)
Graph shows 110 sts.
Length: 140 rows of graph plus bands = $24^1/_2$" or 61 cm

Back
Using band needles and (C) cast on 90 (100, 110) sts. Rib 3".

On the next purl row increase to 100 (110, 120) sts and change to body needles and stocking stitch (Knit the front facing rows and purl the back facing rows). Use full graph for medium size. Add 5 sts to each side for the larger size and take off 5 sts each side for smaller size. Work all additional sts in the colour of the block next to them.

Continue working until 5 rows from the end. Put the central 18 sts on a holder. Work 2 tog at the neck edge on every row 5 times. Cast off remaining 36 (41, 46) shoulder sts. Work other shoulder to match.

Front
As back until 25 rows from the end. Put central 18 sts on holder. Work two together at the neck edge each front facing row 5 times. Continue straight until front matches the back. Cast off remaining 36 (41,46) shoulder stitches.

Sleeves
Cast on 34 sts , rib 3". Change to body needles and increase to 50 sts. Use centre 50 sts of graph as shown by dotted line. Increase one each edge every 6th row thereafter until desired length, (approximately 80 rows).

Cast off loosely. Make second sleeve the same.

Collar
Pick up and knit 92 sts on circular needles around neck hole, and rib for 6". Cast off, fold in and stitch.

Finishing
Sew side seams and sleeve seams. Set sleeves deeply. Sew tails and press gently.

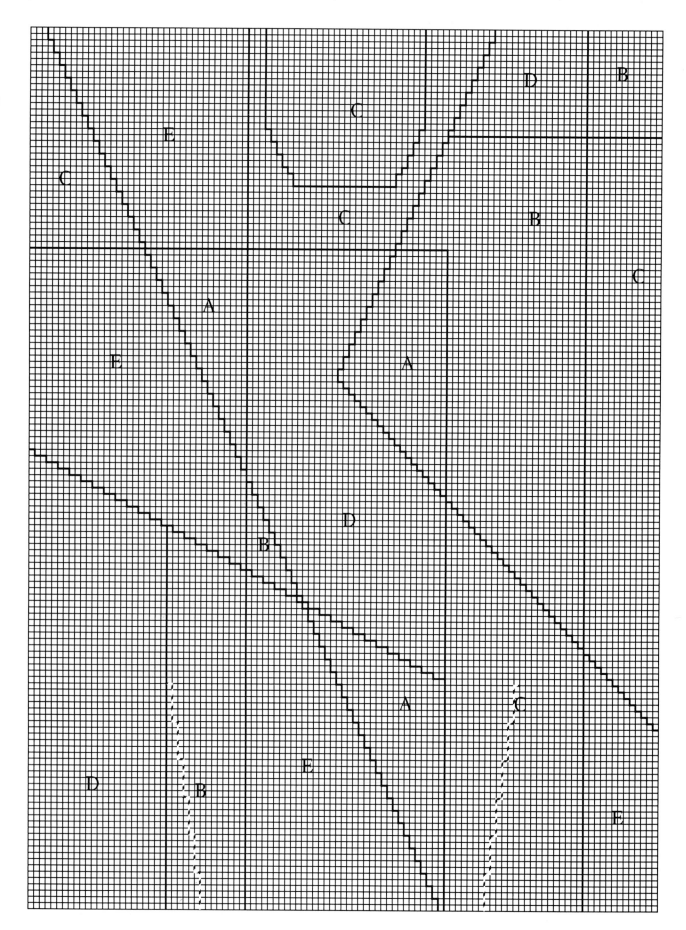

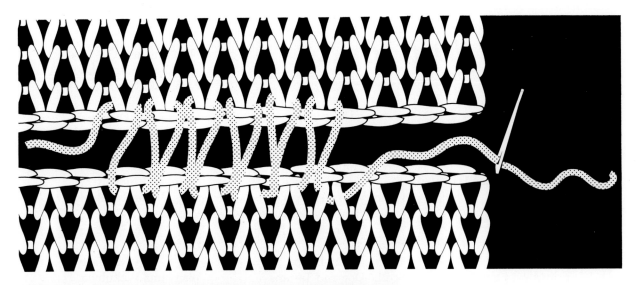

Weaving Method

Up through the Bar Method

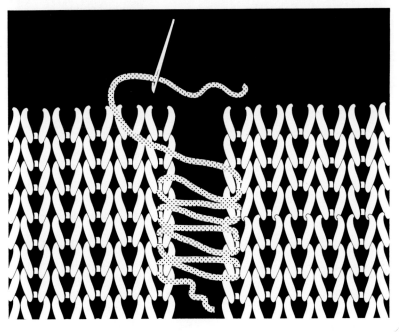

Fairisle

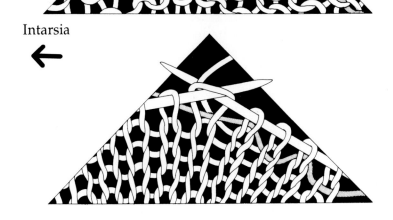

Intarsia

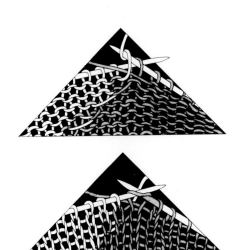

111

Thank you to...

Models

Tropical Fish
> Marissa Strickland

Watercolour Squares
> Mark Strassner

Floral Encore
> Laura Valderas

Contentment Coat
> Erin Shevaughn Frisby

1920's Golf
> Kimberly Pfeiffer

Bold and Brilliant
> Danielle Babcock

Race Winner
> Katie Durgin

Shades of Jade Argyle
> Adam J. Richter

Valley Flowers
> Sarah Stang
> Kim Pfeiffer

New England
> Kara Nunley

Fabiola Lily
> Kim Pfeiffer

Intersecting Diamonds
> Erin Shevaughn Frisby

Statue Coat
> Marissa Strickland

Cropped Vineyard
> Erin Shevaughn Frisby

Deca Red
(cover) Colleen Crouch

Deca Denim
> Al Scolnik
> Mark Strassner

Wanyama Wakubwa
> Kara Nunley

Energy
> Erin Shevaughn Frishy
> Brad Tyler
> Kara Nunley

(cover) Marissa Strickland

Clear Concept
> Danielle Babcock

Landscape
> Marissa Strickland
> Laura Valderas

Seismograph
> Sarah Briscoe

Country Garden Vest
(cover) Laura Valderas
> Brenda Warshauer

Pyramid
> Sarah Biscoe

Scottie Dog and Tartans
> Danielle Babcock

Find the Flag
> Suzanne Robinson

Sunset at Sea
> Marissa Strickland

Shadow Tiles
> Adam J. Richter

Three Sheep and a Camel
> Adam J. Richter

Earth Energy
> Danielle Babcock

Optics
> Sarah Briscoe

Knitters

Tropical Fish
> Joan Becker

Watercolour Squares
> Nancy Hutting

Floral Encore
> Lee Andersen

Contentment
> Maureen Lasek

1920's Golf
> Bolivia

Bold and Brillant
> Katherine Shatzer

Flowers from
> Brenda Durren

Shades of Jades Argyle
> Lois Barger

Valley Flowers
> Joan Becker

New England Full Length Coat
> Joan Becker

New England Car Coat
> Jennifer Almon

Fabiola Lily
> Zelda Simon

Intersecting Diamonds
> Jackie Zipf

Statue
> Erna Mueller

Cropped Vineyard
> Carolyn Brown

Deca Red
> Lee Andersen

Deca Denim
> Kay Mc Carty

Wanyama Wakubwa
> Renee Ashby

Energy in Galway
> Jackie Zipf

Energy in Galway
cotton versions
> Bolivia

Clear Concept
> Kathy Gerstmeyer

Landscape Vest
> Lee Andersen

Siesmograph
> Brenda Durren

Country Garden Vest
> Lee Andersen

Pyramid
> Carolyn Buckingham

Scottie Dog and Tartan
> Agnes Ratcliffe

Find the Flag
> Carol Glorioso

Sunset at Sea
> Lee Andersen / Bolivia

Shadow Tiles
> Michelle Sharp

Three Sheep and a Camel
> Joan Becker

Earth Energy
> Jennifer Barr

Optics
> Adele Snowman

Design & Production

Brickell Graphics
> Sue Brickell
> (410) 442-5658

112